Why Are So Many Christians Confused About Bible Prophecy?

Emanuel T. Franklin

Published by
Mysteries From The Word Of God
Ministries

Why Are So Many Christians
Confused About
Bible Prophecy?

copyright 1999 - 2001, 2019 by Emanuel T. Franklin

Published by:

Mysteries From The Word Of God
Ministries
P.O. Box 6391
Vancouver, WA 98668

Internet:
BookOnProphecy.org

Email:
servant@fastmail.com

Printed in the USA

ISBN 978-0-9711584-1-2

TABLE OF CONTENTS

PREFACE

This is the second edition of Why are So Many Christians Confused About Bible Prophecy? The only changes that have been made between the second edition and the first edition are:
- The cover design was changed.
- The website and email information has been updated.
- Ordering information for audio tapes was removed.
- A blank space was removed in one Bible scripture reference.
- Page numbers and references to pages were changed.

No other changes have been made to this book.

INTRODUCTION

This book was written to put Jesus Christ back in His proper place - at the head of the church.

As Paul said in I Corinthians 2:4-5:

And my speech and my preaching was not with enticing words of man's wisdom, but in demonstration of the Spirit and of power: That your faith should not stand in the wisdom of men, but in the power of God.

I pray that this book will convict, encourage and help the growth of the body of Christ in obedience to God's Holy Word.

CHAPTER 1

Why Are So Many Christians Confused About Bible Prophecy?

For God is not the author of confusion, but of peace, as in all churches of the saints. I Corinthians 14:33

Many Are Not Reading From The Holy Bible (Old King James Version Only)

In the mid-1980's the Holy Spirit showed me that the new versions of the Bible (meaning any version other than the Old King James version of the Holy Bible) were not the Holy Word Of God. In Psalm 119:89 it states *"For ever, O Lord, thy word is settled in heaven."* The apostle Paul also says in I Timothy 4:1 *"Now the Spirit speaketh expressly, that in the latter times some shall depart from the faith, giving heed to seducing spirits, and doctrines of devils."* The apostle Paul clearly stated in this scripture that in the last days there would be doctrines of devils which these new versions are fulfilling. For those who don't believe we are in the last days let us look at Acts 2:17. In this scripture the apostle Peter was preaching on the day of Pentecost after Jesus ascended into heaven. He was quoting from the prophet Joel. Acts 2:17 states *"And it shall come to pass in the last days, saith God, I will pour out of my Spirit upon all flesh: and your sons and your daughters shall prophesy, and your young men shall see visions, and your old men shall dream dreams."* This scripture shows the beginning of the last days on the day of Pentecost.

Why is this so important? Without the true Word Of God you cannot study Bible prophecy or anything else in the Holy Bible (Old King James version) without compromising the integrity of Scripture.

The NIV has 64,098 less words than the KJV[1]. Many verses in the KJV have been omitted entirely from the new versions. Others have been changed entirely or have been moved from the body of the scripture to mere footnotes. For those readers who are unaware of this, here are some examples comparing the King James Version of the Holy Bible (abbreviated as KJV) with the New International Version (NIV), the New Revised Standard Version (NRSV) and the New Jerusalem Bible (NJB).

The first example is I John 5:7. This is an example of how the new versions have eliminated the three Persons of the Trinity.

For there are three that bear record in heaven, the Father, the Word, and the Holy Ghost: and these three are one. (KJV)

For there are three that testify. (NIV)

There are three that testify. (NRSV)
So there are three witnesses. (NJB)

The second example is Matthew 18:11. This is an example of how the new versions are eliminating scriptures.

For the Son of man is come to save that which was lost. (KJV) (This scripture is omitted from the body of text in the NIV. It is referenced in a footnote).

(This scripture is omitted from the body of text in the NRSV. It is referenced in a footnote).

(This scripture is omitted from the body of text in the NJB. It is referenced in a footnote).

The third example is Daniel 3:25. This scripture shows the Son of God, Jesus, delivering Shadrach, Meshach and Abednego from the fiery furnace. The other versions twist this scripture and blaspheme God.

He answered and said, Lo, I see four men loose, walking in the midst of the fire, and they have no hurt; and the form of the fourth is like the Son of God. (KJV)

He said, "Look! I see four men walking around in the fire, unbound and unharmed, and the fourth looks like a son of the gods." (NIV) (This is absolute blasphemy).

He replied, "But I see four men unbound, walking in the middle of the fire, and they are not hurt; and the fourth has the appearance of a god." (NRSV) (This is also absolute blasphemy).

"But", he went on, "I can see four men walking free in the heart of the fire and quite unharmed! And the fourth looks like a child of the gods!" (NJB) (This is also absolute blasphemy).

We don't have the space to fully discuss this issue in this book. For more information on the subject I encourage you to read a book by G.A. Riplinger titled "New Age Bible Versions" (copyright 1993, ISBN 0-9635845-0-2). This book shows how Satan has used these new versions to change the Word Of God, and how he is deceiving many Christians with these new versions as he deceived Eve from the beginning.

From this point on, when you see "Holy Bible" in this book, it is referring to only the Old King James version of the Holy Bible.

We Must Rightly Divide The Word Of God With Two Or Three Witnesses

In studying Bible prophecy or anything in the Holy Bible it is very important that you get two or three witnesses. II Corinthians 13:1 states *"This is the third time I am coming to you. In the mouth of two or three witnesses shall every word be established."* Psalm 62:11 says *"God hath spoken once; twice have I heard this; that power belongeth unto God."* II Timothy 2:15 states *"Study to show thyself approved unto God, a workman that needeth not to be ashamed, rightly dividing the word of truth."* We must rightly divide the Word of God with two or three witnesses in any studying of the Holy Bible.

Let's look at one example showing what these scriptures mean. In Revelation 13:2 it states *"And the beast which I saw was like unto a leopard, and his feet were as the feet of a bear, and his mouth as the mouth of a lion: and the dragon gave him his power, and his seat, and great authority."* Notice the last portion of this scripture *"and the dragon gave him his power"*. Who is the dragon? Revelation 12:9 states *"And the great dragon was cast out, that old serpent, called the Devil, and*

Satan, which deceiveth the whole world: he was cast out into the earth, and his angels were cast out with him." Revelation 20:2 states" *And he laid hold on the dragon, that old serpent, which is the Devil, and Satan, and bound him a thousand years."* We see in this example how the word "dragon" was used in three scripture verses and explained in two of the verses who the dragon is which is the Devil and Satan.

Many Are Relating The Return Of Jesus Christ To The Time Of His Birth Instead Of To The Time Of His Death

In II Peter 3:8 it states *"But, beloved, be not ignorant of this one thing, that one day is with the Lord as a thousand years, and a thousand years as one day."* In Psalm 90:4 it states *"For a thousand years in thy sight are but as yesterday when it is past, and as a watch in the night."* In looking at these two scriptures, God's word establishes a meaning in some passages of scripture that one day is with the Lord as a thousand years and a thousand years as one day. In the week of creation, told in the book of Genesis Chapter 1, we see that God created everything in the first six days and rested on the seventh day. In relating to these previous scriptures we are coming to the close of the six thousandth year since man was created on the earth and the Bible says how God rested on the seventh day and how we will reign with Christ a thousand years. In Revelation 20:6 *"Blessed and holy is he that hath part in the first resurrection: on such the second death hath no power, but they shall be priests of God and of Christ, and shall reign with him a thousand years."*

Looking at the first six days of creation more closely, on the fourth day God created the sun, moon and the stars. Genesis 1:14-16 states *"And God said, Let there be lights in the firmament of the heaven to divide the day from the night; and let them be for signs, and for seasons, and for days, and years: And let them be for lights in the firmament of the heaven to give light upon the earth: and it was so. And God made two great lights; the greater light to rule the day, and the lesser light to rule the night: he made the stars also.*" And four thousand years later Jesus Christ came on the earth. Malachi 4:2 states *"But unto you that fear my name shall the Sun of righteousness arise with healing in his wings; and ye shall go forth, and grow up as calves of the stall."* Notice the word Sun as describing Jesus Christ. In Revelation 1:16 when John was describing Jesus, it states "*And he had in his right hand seven stars: and out of his mouth went a sharp two edged sword: and his countenance was as the sun shineth in his strength.*" Also, in Revelation 21:23 it states "*And the city had no need of the sun, neither of the moon, to shine in it: for the glory of God did lighten it, and the Lamb is the light thereof.*" We know that Jesus is the Light of the World and from the two other passages in the book of Revelation how his countenance and the Lamb (The Lamb is symbolic of Jesus) is the light for the New Jerusalem.

Now let's look at the birth of Jesus Christ. The scriptures show when Jesus was really born. Matthew 2:1-4, 7-8 state *"Now when Jesus was born in Bethlehem of Judaea in the days of Herod the king, behold, there came wise men from the east to Jerusalem, saying, Where is he that is born King of the Jews? for we have seen his star in the east, and are come to worship him. When Herod the king had heard these things, he was troubled, and all Jerusalem with him. And when he had gathered all the chief priests and the scribes of the people together, he demanded of them where Christ should be born. . . . Then Herod, when he had privily called the wise men, inquired of them diligently what time the star appeared. And he sent them to Bethlehem, and said, Go and search diligently for the young child; and when ye have found him, bring me word again, that I may come and worship him also."* But we know from the scriptures that king Herod did not want to worship Jesus but destroy him. Matthew 2:16, 19-20 state *"Then Herod, when he saw that he was mocked of the wise men, was exceeding wroth, and sent forth, and slew all the children that were in Bethlehem, and in all the coasts thereof, from two years old and under, according to the time which he had diligently inquired of the wise men. . . . But when Herod was dead, behold, an angel of the Lord appeared in a dream to Joseph in Egypt, Saying, Arise, and take the young child and his mother, and go into the land of Israel:for they are dead which sought the young child's life."* History tells us that king Herod died March 13th, 4 B.C. (2). We can find out the time of Jesus Christ's birth if we look at the date of the death of Herod and look at Matthew 2:16 which tells us about his decree to kill all children 2 years old and under. This would take us back to March 13th, 6 B.C. We know that Jesus Christ was on the earth for 33-1/2 years and died on the week of Passover or Feast of unleavened bread which was during the month Abib or Nisan (which is during March or April). From this we see that Jesus Christ would be born in the October or November month in the year 5 B.C.

Now that we know the birth of Jesus Christ was in October or November of 5 B.C., we see that in 1995 we have already past two thousand years since his birth. This is one of the reasons for much of the confusion about the year 2000. From the birth of Christ we can get the death of Jesus Christ if we add 33-1/2 years to His birth. This would take us to March or April, in the year 28 A.D. If we add two thousand years to the date of His death we get 2028 A.D.

In Chapter 5 titled "What Prophecies Must Be Fulfilled Before Jesus Christ's Return," we will show the prophecies which need to be fulfilled before Jesus Christ will return.

We Must Always Include The Nation Of Israel In Prophecy

In studying Bible prophecy, we must always look at God's chosen people and the nation of Israel. In Matthew 24:3 the disciples questioned Jesus about the sign of his coming and the end of the world. It states *"And as he sat upon the mount of Olives, the disciples came unto him privately, saying, Tell us, when shall these things be? and what shall be the sign of thy coming, and of the end of the world?"* In verses 32 through 34, Jesus gave us a parable of Israel describing the last generation when everything would be fulfilled. In Matthew 24:32-34 Jesus says *"Now learn a parable of the fig tree; When his branch is yet tender, and putteth forth leaves, ye know that summer is nigh: So likewise ye, when ye shall see all these things, know that it is near, even at the doors. Verily I say unto you, This generation shall not pass, till all these things be fulfilled."* In verse 32 the fig tree is the nation of Israel. Hosea and Jeremiah speak about first ripe or figs which are in a fig tree. In Hosea 9:10a it says *"I found Israel like grapes in the wilderness; I saw your fathers as the first ripe in the fig tree at her first time:..."* and Jeremiah 24:5 *"Thus saith the Lord, the God of Israel; Like these good figs, so will I acknowledge them that are carried away captive of Judah, whom I have sent out of this place into the land of the Chaldeans for their good."* Israel became a nation in May 1948 and this was sign to the world of just how close we are to the return of Jesus Christ. Jesus said *"When his branch is yet tender, and putteth forth leaves, ye know that summer is nigh. "(Matthew 24:32)* The nation of Israel grew and in June 1967 after the six day war Israel made Jerusalem it's capital and took over other parts of land. In verse 33, Jesus said *"So likewise ye, when ye shall see all these things, know that it is near, even at the doors."* The things Jesus was talking about are in Matthew chapter 24:5-8. *"For many shall come in my name, saying, I am Christ; and shall deceive many. And ye shall hear of wars and rumours of wars: see that ye be not troubled: for all these things must come to pass, but the end is not yet. For nation shall rise against nation, and kingdom against kingdom: and there shall be famines, and pestilences, and earthquakes, in divers places. All these are the beginning of sorrows."* In verse 34, Jesus said *"Verily I say unto you, This generation shall not pass, till all these things be fulfilled."*

In looking at the time of a generation, God moved in 40 years in dealing with the children of Israel. In Acts 7:23-34 it says *"And when he was full forty years old, it came into his heart to visit his brethren the children of Israel. And seeing one of them suffer wrong, he defended him, and avenged him that was oppressed, and smote the Egyptian: For he supposed his brethren would have understood how that God by his hand would deliver them: but they understood not. And the next day he showed himself unto them as they strove, and would have set them at one again, saying, Sirs, ye are brethren; why do ye wrong one to another? But he that did his neighbour wrong thrust him away, saying, Who made thee a ruler and a judge over us? Wilt thou kill me, as thou diddest the Egyptian yesterday? Then fled Moses at this saying, and was a stranger in the land of Madian, where he begat two sons. And when forty years were expired, there appeared to him in the wilderness of mount Sina an angel of the Lord in a flame of fire in a bush. When Moses saw it, he wondered at the sight: and as he drew near to behold it, the voice of the Lord came unto him, Saying, I am the God of thy fathers, the God of Abraham, and the God of Isaac, and the God of Jacob. Then Moses trembled, and durst not behold. Then said the Lord to him, Put off thy shoes from thy feet: for the place where thou standest is holy ground. I have seen, I have seen the affliction of my people which is in Egypt, and I have heard their groaning, and am come down to deliver them. And now come, I will send thee into Egypt."* In these passages, we see Moses visiting his brethren the children of Israel at 40 years old and at 80 years old God speaking to Moses to deliver the children of Israel from Egypt. And last we see Moses at 120 years old when the children of Israel were at the promised land. In Deuteronomy 34:4-7 *"And the Lord said unto him, This is the land which I sware unto Abraham, unto Isaac, and unto Jacob, saying, I will give it unto thy seed: I have caused thee to see it with thine eyes, but thou shalt not go over thither. So Moses the servant of the Lord died there in the land of Moab, according to the word of the Lord. And he buried him in a valley in the land of Moab, over against Beth-peor: but no man knoweth of his sepulchre unto this day. And Moses was an hundred and twenty years old when he died: his eye was not dim, nor his natural force abated."* We see from the scriptures in the book of Acts and Deuteronomy that a generation in God's time with the children of Israel is 40 years.

The Lord Jesus Christ spoke to me on October 16, 1997. He said "This is the last generation." As we said before a generation is 40 years. The Lord Jesus gave me the meaning and time frame relating to Israel and that time frame is from 1988 to 2028. At the time the Lord Jesus Christ gave me the word almost ten years had already past. Anytime you get a word from the Lord it must be confirmed in scripture. I have already explained that a generation in God is 40 years when relating to His chosen people. Also, we can see from the last sub-topic on Jesus Christ's return relating to his death, the year 2028 is exactly two thousand years after the Lord Jesus Christ's death which gives us another confirmation of what the Lord told me in October 16, 1997. What does this mean? As Jesus said in Matthew 24:34 *"Verily I say unto you, This generation shall not pass, till all these things be fulfilled."*

We Must Be Like The People At Berea And Search The Scriptures Daily Whether Those Things Are So

Acts 17:10-11 says *"And the brethren immediately sent away Paul and Silas by night unto Berea: who coming thither went into the synagogue of the Jews. These were more noble than those in Thessalonica, in that they received the word with all readiness of mind, and searched the scriptures daily, whether those things were so."* This was the apostle Paul, who we know to be one of the greatest and most humble apostle to ever walk the face of the earth, with the prophet Silas. Even though these were both great men of God, the people of Berea didn't just take Paul and Silas at their word. The Bereans searched the scriptures daily, whether those things were so. If this was what Christians did today, there would not be so much confusion in the church and with Bible prophecy. But in today's world, when we hear a speaker on Christian television or radio, the host spends several minutes listing all the education of the speaker and how many books he or she has written to try to give the speaker some credibility on the topic being discussed. Then many come on and speak things that not only are not the truth of God's word but are not even in the Holy Bible. You say how could this happen , Paul spoke about this time in II Timothy 4:3-4 which states *"For the time will come when they will not endure sound doctrine; but after their own lusts shall they heap to themselves teachers, having itching ears; And they shall turn away their ears from the truth, and shall be turned unto fables."* The apostle Paul also said concerning the last days in II Timothy 3:7 *"Ever learning, and never able to come to the knowledge of the truth."* We must be careful as Christians to never just accept what someone says, but to verify it with the Word Of God as the Bereans did. In Chapter 2 titled "Let No

Man Deceive You" we will go into more detail concerning these false doctrines.

We Must Never Add Or Take Away From The Word Of God

The book of Revelation makes a very powerful statement concerning adding or taking away from the Word of God. It says in Revelation 22:18-19 *"For I testify unto every man that heareth the words of the prophecy of this book, If any man shall add unto these things, God shall add unto him the plagues that are written in this book: And if any man shall take away from the words of the book of this prophecy, God shall take away his part out of the book of life, and out of the holy city, and from the things which are written in this book."* So for those people who say we don't have to agree on prophecy, that only salvation matters, the Holy Bible is clear if anyone adds to this book God shall add unto him the plagues that are written in this book. Or if any man takes away from this book, God shall take away his part out of the book of life, and of the holy city, and from the things which are written in this book.

The apostle Paul said in Galatians 1:11-12 *"But I certify you, brethren, that the gospel which was preached of me is not after man. For I neither received it of man, neither was I taught it, but by the revelation of Jesus Christ."* What a bold and profound statement the apostle Paul made that the messages he preaches come from the Lord Jesus Christ. How sad it is today, that so many messages preached from the pulpit today are from men and not God. In Titus 1:14 it says *"Not giving heed to Jewish fables, and commandments of men, that turn from the truth."* Notice when messages preached are from men and not Jesus Christ it turns the people from the truth of God's Holy Word unto fables or heresies.

CHAPTER 2

Let No Man Deceive You

Let no man deceive you by any means: for that day shall not come, expect there come a falling away first, and that man of sin be revealed, the son of perdition;
II Thessalonians 2:3

This chapter examines the false doctrines that have infiltrated the church today.

The Pre-Rapture or First Trumpet Message

There are many, many ministers preaching about and Christians talking about what they call the Pre-Rapture or First Trumpet. The"Pre-Rapture" message states that Jesus is coming at any moment to deliver all Christians from this earth and the coming persecution. The "First Trumpet" message basically states that when the First trumpet sounds that the church will be caught away and will not have to endure any persecution. But if you look at the Holy Bible you will **not** find a scripture that states **"the First Trumpet sounds and the church is caught away to be with Jesus."** This is one of the most dangerous messages preached today, and many do not realize that it is not even in the Holy Bible. This message is mainly popular in countries like the United States where Christians are not being persecuted (now). The "Pre-Rapture" or "First Trumpet" message would never be accepted in countries like China and Egypt where Christians are being heavily persecuted. This ministry has sent out thirty-six letters to different ministries (churches, radio and Christian television) about the false "Pre-Rapture or First Trumpet" doctrine and only one ministry changed it's message to match what the scriptures are saying in the Holy Bible. The truth of God's Holy Word is not popular in today's Laodicean church. God told us about this day in the book of Amos. Amos 8:11 says *"Behold, the days come, saith the Lord God, that I will send a famine in the land, not a famine of bread, nor a thirst for water, but of hearing the words of the Lord."* The apostle Paul said in the last days that people would turn their ears from the truth unto fables. In II Timothy 4:3-4 it states *"For the time will come when they will not endure sound doctrine; but after their own lusts shall they heap to themselves teachers, having itching ears; And they shall turn away their ears from the truth, and shall be turned unto fables."* To tell people that Jesus Christ can come at any moment and that no more prophecies need to be fulfilled is a lie from the devil and a heresy. Notice in Galatians 5:19-21 it says *"Now the works of the flesh are manifest, which are these; Adultery, fornication, uncleanness, lasciviousness, idolatry, witchcraft, hatred, variance, emulations, wrath, strife, seditions, heresies, envying, murders, drunkenness, revellings, and such like: of the which I tell you in time past, that they which do such things shall not inherit the kingdom of God."* We can see from this scripture in Galatians that those who speak heresies will not inherit the kingdom of God. In Titus 3:10-11 it says *"A man that is an heretic after the first and second admonition reject; Knowing that he that is such is subverted, and sinneth, being condemned of himself".* We can see from this scripture in Titus that if one who has been corrected about heresies continues to reject the correction in the Word of God, that this person is condemned. If you are a minister or Christian who is reading this for the first time and you have been preaching or teaching this lie then repent and ask Jesus Christ for forgiveness. I John 1:9 says *"If we confess our sins, he is faithful and just to forgive us our sins, and to cleanse us from all unrighteousness."*

Paul told us that Jesus would come for His people at **the last trumpet.** I Corinthians 15:51-52 states *"Behold, I show you a mystery; We shall not all sleep, but we shall all be changed, in a moment, in the twinkling of an eye, at the last trump; for the trumpet shall sound, and the dead shall be raised incorruptible, and we shall be changed."*

In Chapter 5 titled "What Prophecies Must Be Fulfilled Before Jesus Christ's Return," I will go into much more detail about the last trumpet.

The Pensacola /Toronto Revival Or Falling Away

Many Christians have said that a revival and outpouring of God's Holy Spirit is taking place in Pensacola, Florida and Toronto, Ontario (Canada). In II Corinthians 11:1-5,13-15 it says *"Would to God ye could bear with me a little in my folly: and indeed bear with me. For I am jealous over you with godly jealousy: for I have espoused you to one husband, that I may present you as a chaste virgin to Christ. But I fear, lest by any means, as the serpent beguiled Eve through his subtlety, so your minds should be corrupted from the simplicity that is in Christ. For if he that cometh preacheth another Jesus, whom we have not preached, or if ye receive another spirit, which ye have not received, or another gospel, which ye have not accepted, ye might well bear with him. ... For such are false apostles, deceitful workers, transforming themselves into the apostles of Christ. And no marvel; for Satan himself is transformed into an angel of light. Therefore it is no great thing if his ministers also be transformed as the ministers of righteousness; whose end shall be according to their works."* The apostle Paul was concerned about false teachers which existed in his time and exist today. Notice in verse 4 Paul said three things about these false teachers, first *"For if he that cometh preacheth another Jesus"*, second *"or if ye receive another spirit"* and third *"or another gospel,"*.

I want share with you comments and direct quotes from two videos titled "Kenneth Hagin and the Spirit of the Serpent" and "Pensacola Impartations." These videos were produced by Pastor Joseph Chambers, a Pentecostal preacher of fifty years.

I heard an interview with Pastor Joseph Chambers and heard excerpts from these videos myself. These comments are quoted from a brochure produced by Southwest Radio Church about these videos.

These comments are from the video titled "Kenneth Hagin and the Spirit of the Serpent."

"...tongue slithering in and out like a serpent's"
"...hissing and laughing insanely"
"People in the congregation slithering down feet first out of their seats"
"Guru-type influences over the audience"
"You will also hear (a well-known minister's) support the following: Levitation or bodies suspended in the air. People in trances that weighed incredible amounts."

These comments are from the video titled "Pensacola Impartations."

"The manifestations are worse than Toronto! Young girls shaking so violently they appear bizarre and epileptic."
" Beatles music that alters consciousness."
" Guided imagery praying."

(Quote from a minister) "We have had people, agnostics, God-haters, businessmen come to our meetings and they've been thrown through the air up against a wall and hit the ground when we shook their hand."
(Quote from another minister) "My wife can't even do her housework, I have to start dressing at 4:30 ... took 30 minutes to put on my socks!"[1].

From these quotes and comments it is evident that this is no revival but a falling away from the truth of the gospel of Jesus Christ. These ministers are being deceived by the devil himself. If you have in any way supported this abomination, you must repent immediately and pray for the other people to be delivered from this deception.

Fallen Angels And Doctrines Of Demons

In I Timothy 4:1 it says *"Now the Spirit speaketh expressly, that in the latter times some shall depart from the faith, giving heed to seducing spirits, and doctrines of devils."* The apostle Paul also told us in Galatians 1:6-8 *"I marvel that ye are so soon removed from him that called you into the grace of Christ unto another gospel: Which is not another; but there be some that trouble you, and would pervert the gospel of Christ. But though we, or an angel from heaven, preach any other gospel unto you than that which we have preached unto you, let him be accursed."* From these scriptures in I Timothy and Galatians we see fallen angels or demons deceiving people as seducing spirits and doctrine of devils. What is a fallen angel or demon? When Satan was cast out of heaven, a third of the angels went with him. These are called fallen angels, or demons. In Revelation 12:3-4 and 12:9 it states *"And there appeared another wonder in heaven; and behold a great red dragon, having seven heads and ten horns, and seven crowns upon his heads. And his tail drew the third part of the stars of heaven,*

Page 17

and did cast them to the earth: and the dragon stood before the woman which was ready to be delivered for to devour her child as soon as it was born....And the great dragon was cast out, that old serpent, called the Devil, and Satan, which deceiveth the whole world: he was cast out into the earth, and his angels were cast out with him." The great red dragon, spoken of in verse 9, is the Devil and Satan. Verse 4 says his tail (referring to Satan) drew the third part of the stars and did cast them to the earth. In Revelation 1:20 it tells us that the stars are symbolic of angels. It states *"The mystery of the seven stars which thou sawest in my right hand, and the seven golden candlesticks. The seven stars are the angels of the seven churches: and the seven candlesticks which thou sawest are the seven churches."*

The scriptures show how demons can deceive people. A lying spirit was used to deceive king Ahab. King Ahab was more evil than all of his predecessors. I Kings 16:33 says *"And Ahab made a grove; and Ahab did more to provoke the Lord God of Israel to anger than all the kings of Israel that were before him."* He didn't want to hear a word from a true prophet of God, Micaiah. In I Kings 22:5-8 it says *"And Jehoshaphat said unto the king of Israel, Inquire, I pray thee, at the word of the Lord today. Then the king of Israel gathered the prophets together, about four hundred men, and said unto them, Shall I go against Ramoth-gilead to battle, or shall I forbear? And they said, Go up; for the Lord shall deliver it into the hand of the king. And Jehoshaphat said, Is there not here a prophet of the Lord besides, that we might inquire of him? And the king of Israel said unto Jehoshaphat, There is yet one man, Micaiah the son of Imlah, by whom we may inquire of the Lord: but I hate him; for he doth not prophesy good concerning me, but evil. And Jehoshaphat said, Let not the king say so."* Then Micaiah, the true prophet of God, told king Ahab how a lying spirit was used to deceive him. I Kings 22:19-23 says *"And he said, Hear thou therefore the word of the Lord: I saw the Lord sitting on his throne, and all the host of heaven standing by him on his right hand and on his left. And the Lord said, Who shall persuade Ahab, that he may go up and fall at Ramoth-gilead? And one said on this manner, and another said on that manner. And there came forth a spirit, and stood before the Lord, and said, I will persuade him. And the Lord said unto him, Wherewith? And he said, I will go forth, and I will be a lying spirit in the mouth of all his prophets. And he said, Thou shalt persuade him, and prevail also, go forth, and do so. Now therefore, behold, the Lord hath put a lying spirit in the mouth of all these thy prophets, and the Lord hath spoken evil concerning thee."* We see king Ahab and many people today would rather hear from a false prophet than from a true prophet of God. Ahab's decision to listen to false prophets instead of God's prophet lead to his death.

Many Christians are being deceived today. The first two topics of this chapter described how people are being deceived through the Pre-Rapture or First Trumpet Message and through the Pensacola /Toronto Falling Away.

How can we discern the difference between a message from God or a deceptive message from a fallen angel? In I John 4:1 it states *"Beloved, Believe not every spirit, but try the spirits whether they are of God: because many false prophets are gone out into the world."* In Galatians 1:8 it says *"But though we, or an angel from heaven, preach any other gospel unto you than that which we have preached unto you, let him be accursed."* God's Holy angels, the Holy Spirit and the Word of God will always agree. We must pray for these people who are being deceived that they might be delivered from these seducing spirits and doctrine of devils.

In Chapter 7 titled "God's Holy Angels," we will show how God still does use His angels in helping His people.

CHAPTER 3

The Door Is Closing To The Gentiles

For I would not, brethren, that ye should be ignorant of this mystery, lest ye should be wise in your own conceits; that blindness in part is happened to Israel, until the fulness of the Gentiles be come in.
Romans 11:25

Soon the door will close to the Gentiles which means that the time will come when no more Gentiles can be saved. This chapter traces the gospel from the time it was first brought to the Jewish people to the regathering of Israel and the time when no more Gentiles can be saved. If you are not saved, please ask Jesus to come into your heart. (See "Come While The Door Is Still Open For The Gentiles" on page 36 of this chapter and also chapter 10, "What Can A Christian Do?")

The Gospel To Be Preached First To The Jewish People

In the gospel of Matthew chapter 10, Jesus told the disciples to only preach to the Jewish people. In Matthew 10:1-8 it says

"1 And when he had called unto him his twelve disciples, he gave them power against unclean spirits, to cast them out, and to heal all manner of sickness and all manner of disease. 2 Now the names of the twelve apostles are these; The first, Simon, who is called Peter, and Andrew his brother; James the son of Zebedee, and John his brother; 3 Philip, and Bartholomew; Thomas, and Matthew the publican; James the son of Alphaeus, and Lebbaeus, whose surname was Thaddaeus; 4 Simon the Canaanite, and Judas Iscariot, who also betrayed him. 5 These twelve Jesus sent forth, and commanded them, saying, Go not into the way of the Gentiles, and into any city of the Samaritans enter ye not: 6 But go rather to the lost sheep of the house of Israel. 7 And as ye go, preach, saying, The kingdom of heaven is at hand. 8 Heal the sick, cleanse the lepers, raise the dead, cast out devils: freely ye have received, freely give." Jesus spoke again concerning preaching to the children of Israel as a woman of Canaan came to him. In Matthew 15:21-24 it says *"21 Then Jesus went thence, and departed into the coasts of Tyre and Sidon. 22 And, behold, a woman of Canaan came out of the same coasts, and cried unto him, saying, Have mercy on me, O Lord, thou Son of David; my daughter is grievously vexed with a devil. 23 But he answered her not a word. And his disciples came and besought him, saying, Send her away; for she crieth after us. 24 But he answered and said, I am not sent but unto the lost sheep of the house of Israel."*

The Jewish People Demand The Death Of Jesus Christ

Jesus Christ stood before Pontius Pilate and Pilate found no fault in him. But the people cried out *"Let him be crucified"*. In Matthew 27:11-26 it says *"11 And Jesus stood before the governor: and the governor asked him, saying, Art thou the King of the Jews? And Jesus said unto him, Thou sayest. 12*

And when he was accused of the chief priests and elders, he answered nothing. 13 Then said Pilate unto him, Hearest thou not how many things they witness against thee? 14 And he answered him to never a word; insomuch that the governor marvelled greatly. 15 Now at that feast the governor was wont to release unto the people a prisoner, whom they would. 16 And they had then a notable prisoner, called Barabbas. 17 Therefore when they were gathered together, Pilate said unto them, Whom will ye that I release unto you? Barabbas, or Jesus which is called Christ? 18 For he knew that for envy they had delivered him. 19 When he was set down on the judgment seat, his wife sent unto him, saying, Have thou nothing to do with that just man: for I have suffered many things this day in a dream because of him. 20 But the chief priests and elders persuaded the multitude that they should ask Barabbas, and destroy Jesus. 21 The governor answered and said unto them, Whether of the twain will ye that I release unto you? They said, Barabbas. 22 Pilate saith unto them, What shall I do then with Jesus which is called Christ? They all say unto him, Let him be crucified. 23 And the governor said, Why, what evil hath he done? But they cried out the more, saying, Let him be crucified. 24 When Pilate saw that he could prevail nothing, but that rather a tumult was made, he took water, and washed his hands before the multitude, saying, I am innocent of the blood of this just person: see ye to it. 25 Then answered all the people, and said, His blood be on us, and on our children. 26 Then released he Barabbas unto them: and when he had scourged Jesus, he delivered him to be crucified." Notice in verse 24 how Pilate washed his hands before the multitude saying *"I am innocent of the blood of this just person: see ye to it."* But the people responded saying *"His blood be on us, and on our children."* The apostle Peter, preaching on the day of Pentecost, acknowledges that the Jewish people demanded the death of Jesus. In Acts 2:36 it says *"Therefore let all the house of Israel know assuredly, that God hath made that same Jesus, whom ye have crucified, both Lord and Christ."*

Jesus Christ's Great Commission And Ascension

After Jesus Christ arose from the dead He was seen by the apostles and He told them to wait for the promise of the Holy Ghost. In Acts 1:2-9 it says *"2 Until the day in which he was taken up, after that he through the Holy Ghost had given commandments unto the apostles whom he had chosen: 3 To whom also he shewed himself alive after his passion by many infallible proofs, being seen of them forty days, and speaking of the things pertaining to the kingdom of God: 4 And, being assembled together with them, commanded them that they should not depart from Jerusalem, but wait for the promise of the Father, which, saith he, ye have heard of me. 5 For John truly baptized with water; but ye shall be baptized with the Holy Ghost not many days hence. 6 When they therefore were come together, they asked of him, saying, Lord, wilt thou at this time restore again the kingdom to Israel? 7 And he said unto them, It is not for you to know the times or the seasons, which the Father hath put in his own power. 8 But ye shall receive power, after that the Holy Ghost is come upon you: and ye shall be witnesses unto me both in Jerusalem, and in all Judaea, and in Samaria, and unto the uttermost part of the earth. 9 And when he had spoken these things, while they beheld, he was taken up; and a cloud received him out of their sight."* In verse 8 Jesus told the disciples that after they received the Holy Ghost they would be witnesses not only in Jerusalem but also to the uttermost part of the earth.

The Day Of Pentecost (The Start Of The Church)

When the day of Pentecost came they were all filled with the Holy Ghost and this was the start of the Church. The church grew as the apostle Peter preached on the day of Pentecost and the church added about three thousand souls. Chapter 2 of Acts shows this great event. In Acts 2:1-47 it says *"1 And when the day of Pentecost was fully come, they were all with one accord in one place. 2 And suddenly there came a sound from heaven as of a rushing mighty wind, and it filled all the house where they were sitting. 3 And there appeared unto them cloven tongues like as of fire, and it sat upon each of them. 4 And they were all filled with the Holy Ghost, and began to speak with other tongues, as the Spirit gave them utterance. 5 And there were dwelling at Jerusalem Jews, devout men, out of every nation under heaven. 6 Now when this was noised abroad, the multitude came together, and were confounded, because that every man heard them speak in his own language. 7 And they were all amazed and marvelled, saying one to another, Behold, are not all these which speak Galilaeans? 8 And how hear we every man in our own tongue, wherein we were born? 9 Parthians, and Medes, and Elamites, and the dwellers in Mesopotamia, and in Judaea, and Cappadocia, in Pontus, and Asia, 10 Phrygia, and Pamphylia, in Egypt, and in the parts of Libya about Cyrene, and strangers of Rome, Jews and proselytes, 11 Cretes and Arabians, we do hear them speak in our tongues the wonderful works of God. 12 And they were all amazed, and were in doubt, saying one to another, What meaneth this? 13 Others mocking said, These men are full of new wine. 14 But Peter, standing up with the eleven, lifted up his voice, and said unto them, Ye men of Judaea, and all ye that dwell at Jerusalem, be this known unto you, and hearken to my words: 15 For these are not drunken, as ye suppose, seeing it is but the third hour of the day. 16 But this is that which was spoken by the prophet Joel; 17 And it shall come to pass in the last days, saith God, I will pour out of my Spirit upon all flesh: and your sons and your daughters shall prophesy, and your young men shall see visions, and your old men shall dream dreams: 18 And on my servants and on my handmaidens I will pour out in those days of my Spirit; and they shall prophesy: 19 And I will shew wonders in heaven above, and signs in the earth beneath; blood, and fire, and vapour of smoke: 20 The sun shall be turned into darkness, and the moon into blood, before that great and notable day of the Lord come: 21 And it shall come to pass, that whosoever shall call on the name of the Lord shall be saved. 22 Ye men of Israel, hear these words; Jesus of Nazareth, a man approved of God among you by miracles and wonders and signs, which God did by him in the midst of you, as ye yourselves also know: 23 Him, being delivered by the determinate counsel and foreknowledge of God, ye have taken, and by wicked hands have crucified and slain: 24 Whom God hath raised up, having loosed the pains of death: because it was not possible that he should be holden of it. 25 For David speaketh concerning him, I foresaw the Lord always before my face, for he is on my right hand, that I should not be moved: 26 Therefore did my heart rejoice, and my tongue was glad; moreover also my flesh shall rest in hope: 27 Because thou wilt not leave my soul in hell, neither wilt thou suffer thine Holy One to see corruption. 28 Thou hast made known to me the ways of life; thou shalt make me full of joy with thy countenance. 29 Men and brethren, let me freely speak unto you of the patriarch David, that he is both dead and buried, and his sepulchre is with us unto this day. 30 Therefore being a prophet, and knowing that God had sworn with an oath to him, that of the fruit of his loins, according to the flesh, he would raise up Christ to sit on his throne; 31 He seeing this before spake of the resurrection of Christ, that his soul was not left in hell, neither his flesh did see corruption. 32 This Jesus hath God raised up, whereof we all are witnesses. 33 Therefore being by the right hand of God exalted, and having received of the Father the promise of the Holy Ghost, he hath shed forth this, which ye now see and hear. 34 For David is not ascended into the heavens: but he saith himself, The LORD said unto my Lord, Sit thou on my right hand, 35 Until I make thy foes thy footstool. 36 Therefore let all the house of Israel know assuredly, that God hath made that same Jesus, whom ye have crucified, both Lord and Christ. 37 Now when they heard this, they were pricked in their heart, and said unto Peter and to the rest of the apostles, Men and brethren, what shall we do? 38 Then Peter said unto them, Repent, and be baptized every one of you in the name of Jesus Christ for the remission of sins, and ye shall receive the gift of the Holy Ghost. 39 For the promise is unto you, and to your children, and to all that are afar off, even as many as the Lord our God shall call. 40 And with many other words did he testify and exhort, saying, Save yourselves from this untoward generation. 41 Then they that gladly received his word were baptized: and the same day there were added unto them about three thousand souls. 42 And they continued stedfastly in the apostles' doctrine and fellowship, and in breaking of bread, and in prayers. 43 And fear came upon every soul: and many wonders and signs were done by the apostles. 44 And all that believed were together, and had all things common; 45 And sold their possessions and goods, and parted them to all men, as every man had need. 46 And they, continuing daily with one accord in the temple, and breaking bread from house to house, did eat their meat with gladness and singleness of heart, 47 Praising God, and having favour with all the people. And the Lord added to the church daily such as should be saved."*

The Gentiles Receive The Gift Of The Holy Ghost

After the day of Pentecost the Holy Ghost was poured out on only the Jewish people. Later, as the apostle Peter was preaching to Cornelius he and those at his house were filled with the Holy Ghost. This was the first time the Holy Ghost fell upon Gentiles. In Acts 10:34-48 it says *"34 Then Peter opened his mouth, and said, Of a truth I perceive that God is no respecter of persons: 35 But in every nation he that feareth him, and worketh righteousness, is accepted with him. 36 The word which God sent unto the children of Israel, preaching peace by Jesus Christ: (he is Lord of all:) 37 That word, I say, ye know, which was published throughout all Judaea, and began from Galilee, after the baptism which John preached; 38 How God anointed Jesus of Nazareth with the Holy Ghost and with power: who went about doing good, and healing all that were oppressed of the devil; for God was with him. 39 And we are witnesses of all things which he did both in the land of the Jews, and in Jerusalem; whom they slew and hanged on a tree: 40 Him God raised up the third day, and shewed him openly; 41 Not to all the people, but unto witnesses chosen before of God, even to us, who did eat and drink with him after he rose from the dead. 42 And he commanded us to preach unto the people, and to testify that it is he which was ordained of God to be the Judge of quick and dead. 43 To him give all the prophets witness, that through his name whosoever believeth in him shall receive remission of sins. 44 While Peter yet spake these words, the Holy Ghost fell on all them which heard the word. 45 And they of the circumcision which believed were astonished, as many as came with Peter, because that on the Gentiles also was poured out the gift of the Holy Ghost. 46 For they heard them speak with tongues, and magnify God. Then answered Peter, 47 Can any man forbid water, that these should not be baptized, which have received the Holy Ghost as well as we? 48 And he commanded them to be baptized in the name of the Lord. Then prayed they him to tarry certain days."*

The Jewish People Oppose; Gentiles Believe

As the apostles began to preach to the Gentiles, the Jewish people came against Paul and Barnabas. In Acts 13:44-52 it says *"44 And the next sabbath day came almost the whole city together to hear the word of God. 45 But when the Jews saw the multitudes, they were filled with envy, and spake against those things which were spoken by Paul, contradicting and blaspheming. 46 Then Paul and Barnabas waxed bold, and said, It was necessary that the word of God should first have been spoken to you: but seeing ye put it from you, and judge yourselves unworthy of everlasting life, lo, we turn to the Gentiles. 47 For so hath the Lord commanded us, saying, I have set thee to be a light of the Gentiles, that thou shouldest be for salvation unto the ends of the earth. 48 And when the Gentiles heard this, they were glad, and glorified the word of the Lord: and as many as were ordained to eternal life believed. 49 And the word of the Lord was published throughout all the region. 50 But the Jews stirred up the devout and honourable women, and the chief men of the city, and raised persecution against Paul and Barnabas, and expelled them out of their coasts. 51 But they shook off the dust of their feet against them, and came unto Iconium. 52 And the disciples were filled with joy, and with the Holy Ghost."* The apostle Paul spoke in verse 46 *"Then Paul and Barnabas waxed bold, and said, It was necessary that the word of God should first have been spoken to you: but seeing ye put it from you, and judge yourselves unworthy of everlasting life, lo, we turn to the Gentiles."* This is the time when the Jewish people rejected the gospel and the Gentiles received it.

The Gospel Of Jesus Christ To Be Preached To The Gentiles About 2000 Years

In the gospel of John chapter 4, Jesus spoke to a woman of Samaria and later in this chapter he even visited the Samaritans for two days preaching the kingdom of God. This was very unusual for a Jewish person to speak to the Samaritans but also we can see a prophetic time concerning this event. In John 4:1-30 it says *"1 When therefore the Lord knew how the Pharisees had heard that Jesus made and baptized more disciples than John, 2 (Though Jesus himself baptized not, but his disciples,) 3 He left Judaea, and departed again into Galilee. 4 And he must needs go through Samaria. 5 Then cometh he to a city of Samaria, which is called Sychar, near to the parcel of ground that Jacob gave to his son Joseph. 6 Now Jacob's well was there. Jesus therefore, being wearied with his journey, sat thus on the well: and it was about the sixth hour. 7 There cometh a woman of Samaria to draw water: Jesus saith unto her, Give me to drink. 8 (For his disciples were gone away unto the city to buy meat.) 9 Then saith the woman of Samaria unto him, How is it that thou, being a Jew, askest drink of me, which am a woman of Samaria? for the Jews have no dealings with the Samaritans. 10 Jesus answered and said unto her, If thou knewest the gift of God, and who it is that saith to thee, Give me to drink; thou wouldest have asked of him, and he would have given thee living water. 11 The woman saith unto him, Sir, thou hast nothing to draw with, and the well is deep: from whence then hast thou that living water? 12 Art thou greater than our father Jacob, which gave us the well, and drank thereof himself, and his children, and his cattle? 13 Jesus answered and said unto her, Whosoever drinketh of this water shall thirst again: 14 But whosoever drinketh of the water that I shall give him shall never thirst; but the water that I shall give him shall be in him a well of water springing up into everlasting life. 15 The woman saith unto him, Sir, give me this water, that I thirst not, neither come hither to draw. 16 Jesus saith unto her, Go, call thy husband, and come hither. 17 The woman answered and said, I have no husband. Jesus said unto her, Thou hast well said, I have no husband: 18 For thou hast had five husbands; and he whom thou now hast is not thy husband: in that saidst thou truly. 19 The woman saith unto him, Sir, I perceive that thou art a prophet. 20 Our fathers worshipped in this mountain; and ye say, that in Jerusalem is the place where men ought to worship. 21 Jesus saith unto her, Woman, believe me, the hour cometh, when ye shall neither in this mountain, nor yet at Jerusalem, worship the Father. 22 Ye worship ye know not what: we know what we worship: for salvation is of the Jews. 23 But the hour cometh, and now is, when the true worshippers shall worship the Father in spirit and in truth: for the Father seeketh such to worship him. 24 God is a Spirit: and they that worship him must worship him in spirit and in truth. 25 The woman saith unto him, I know that Messias cometh, which is called Christ: when he is come, he will tell us all things. 26 Jesus saith unto her, I that speak unto thee am he. 27 And upon this came his disciples, and marvelled that he talked with the woman: yet no man said, What seekest thou? or, Why talkest thou with her? 28 The woman then left her waterpot, and went her way into the city, and saith to the men, 29 Come, see a man, which told me all things that ever I did: is not this the Christ? 30 Then they went out of the city, and came unto him.*

John 4:39-45 says *39 And many of the Samaritans of that city believed on him for the saying of the woman, which testified, He told me all that ever I did. 40 So when the Samaritans were come unto him, they besought him that he would tarry with them: and he abode there two days. 41 And many more believed because of his own word; 42 And said unto the woman, Now we believe, not because of thy saying: for we have heard him ourselves, and know that this is indeed the Christ, the Saviour of the world. 43 Now after two days he departed thence, and went into Galilee. 44 For Jesus himself testified, that a prophet hath no honour in his own country. 45 Then when he was come into Galilee, the Galilaeans received him, having seen all the things that he did at Jerusalem at the feast: for they also went unto the feast."* Jesus Christ revealed the sin of the woman of Samaria and she told many in Samaria her testimony about Jesus Christ and many believed on him. Then Jesus Christ stayed with them for two days.

Notice in John 4:40-41 that Jesus Christ stayed with the Samaritans for two days and many more believed on him. In II Peter 3:8 it says *"8 But, beloved, be not ignorant of this one thing, that one day is with the Lord as a thousand years, and a thousand years as one day."* As Jesus Christ was there two day, so we are coming close to the 2000th year since Jesus Christ preached to the people of Samaria. In Acts chapter 15 Simeon spoke how God would visit the Gentiles and take a people for his name. In Acts 15:14 it says *"Simeon hath declared how God at the first did visit the Gentiles, to take out of them a people for his name."*

God To Regather And Restore Israel

God Restoring The Children Of Israel Into Their Own Land

In Ezekiel 36:22-24, God speaks of restoring the children of Israel out of the heathen countries and bringing them into their own land. This has been taking place since May 1948, but there are still many Israelites in the United States and around the world that God will bring into his land again. In Ezekiel 36:22-24 it says

"22 Therefore say unto the house of Israel, Thus saith the Lord GOD; I do not this for your sakes, O house of Israel, but for mine holy name's sake, which ye have profaned among the heathen, whither ye went. 23 And I will sanctify my great name, which was profaned among the heathen, which ye have profaned in the midst of them; and the heathen shall know that I am the LORD, saith the Lord GOD, when I shall be sanctified in you before their eyes. 24 For I will take you from among the heathen, and gather you out of all countries, and will bring you into your own land."

Jesus Christ used a parable of a fig tree to tell us about the restoration of Israel. In Matthew 24:32-34 Jesus said *"32 Now learn a parable of the fig tree; When his branch is yet tender, and putteth forth leaves, ye know that summer is nigh: 33 So likewise ye, when ye shall see all these things, know that it is near, even at the doors. 34 Verily I say unto you, This generation shall not pass, till all these things be fulfilled"* (for more information see "We Must Always Include The Nation Of Israel In Prophecy" in Chapter 1).

The Times Of The Gentiles Fulfilled

The times of the Gentiles were fulfilled when the Jewish people reclaimed Jerusalem from the Gentiles.   In Luke 21:24 it says *"And they shall fall by the edge of the sword, and shall be led away captive into all nations: and Jerusalem shall be trodden down of the Gentiles, until the times of the Gentiles be fulfilled."* This scripture was fulfilled in June 1967 after the Six Day war in the Middle East when Israel took over all of Jerusalem.

The Future Salvation Of Israel

The apostle Paul told us in Romans 11 about the future salvation of Israel. In Romans 11:1-27 it says *"1 I say then, Hath God cast away his people? God forbid. For I also am an Israelite, of the seed of Abraham, of the tribe of Benjamin. 2 God hath not cast away his people which he foreknew. Wot ye not what the scripture saith of Elias? how he maketh intercession to God against Israel, saying, 3 Lord, they have killed thy prophets, and digged down thine altars; and I am left alone, and they seek my life. 4 But what saith the answer of God unto him? I have reserved to myself seven thousand men, who have not bowed the knee to the image of Baal. 5 Even so then at this present time also there is a remnant according to the election of grace. 6 And if by grace, then is it no more of works: otherwise grace is no more grace. But if it be of works, then is it no more grace: otherwise work is no more work. 7 What then? Israel hath not obtained that which he seeketh for; but the election hath obtained it, and the rest were blinded 8 (According as it is written, God hath given them the spirit of slumber, eyes that they should not see, and ears that they should not hear;) unto this day. 9 And David saith, Let their table be made a snare, and a trap, and a stumblingblock, and a recompence unto them: 10 Let their eyes be darkened, that they may not see, and bow down their back alway. 11 I say then, Have they stumbled that they should fall? God forbid: but rather through their fall salvation is come unto the Gentiles, for to provoke them to jealousy. 12 Now if the fall of them be the riches of the world, and the diminishing of them the riches of the Gentiles; how much more their fulness? 13 For I speak to you Gentiles, inasmuch as I am the apostle of the Gentiles, I magnify mine office: 14 If by any means I may provoke to emulation them which are my flesh, and might save some of them. 15 For if the casting away of them be the reconciling of the world, what shall the receiving of them be, but life from the dead? 16 For if the firstfruit be holy, the lump is also holy: and if the root be holy, so are the branches. 17 And if some of the branches be broken off, and thou, being a wild olive tree, wert graffed in among them, and with them partakest of the root and fatness of the olive tree; 18 Boast not against the branches. But if thou boast, thou bearest not the root, but the root thee. 19 Thou wilt say then, The branches were broken off, that I might be graffed in. 20 Well; because of unbelief they were broken off, and thou standest by faith. Be not highminded, but fear: 21 For if God spared not the natural branches, take heed lest he also spare not thee. 22 Behold therefore the goodness and severity of God: on them which fell, severity; but toward thee, goodness, if thou continue in his goodness: otherwise thou also shalt be cut off. 23 And they also, if they abide not still in unbelief, shall be graffed in: for God is able to graff them in again. 24 For if thou wert cut out of the olive tree which is wild by nature, and wert graffed contrary to nature into a good olive tree: how much more shall these, which be the natural branches, be graffed into their own olive tree? 25 For I would not, brethren, that ye should be ignorant of this mystery, lest ye should be wise in your own conceits; that blindness in part is happened to Israel, until the fulness of the Gentiles be come in. 26 And so all Israel shall be saved: as it is written, There shall come out of Sion the Deliverer, and shall turn away ungodliness from Jacob: 27 For this is my covenant unto them, when I shall take away their sins."* In verses 25-27 Paul shows us the time when the fulness of the Gentiles is complete. This is when no other Gentiles can be saved and salvation comes to Israel.

The prophet Ezekiel shows us a similar scripture about the future salvation of the children of Israel. In Ezekiel 36:25-38 it says *"25 Then will I sprinkle clean water upon you, and ye shall be clean: from all your filthiness, and from all your idols, will I cleanse you. 26 A new heart also will I give you, and a new spirit will I put within you: and I will take away the stony heart out of your flesh, and I will give you an heart of flesh. 27 And I will put my spirit within you, and cause you to walk in my statutes, and ye shall keep my judgments, and do them. 28 And ye shall dwell in the land that I gave to your fathers; and ye shall be my people, and I will be your God. 29 I will also save you from all your uncleannesses: and I will call for the corn, and will increase it, and lay no famine upon you. 30 And I will multiply the fruit of the tree, and the increase of the field, that ye shall receive no more reproach of famine among the heathen. 31 Then shall ye remember your own evil ways, and your doings that were not good, and shall lothe yourselves in your own sight for your iniquities and for your abominations. 32 Not for your sakes do I this, saith the Lord GOD, be it known unto you: be ashamed and confounded for your own ways, O house of Israel. 33 Thus saith the Lord GOD; In the day that I shall have cleansed you from all your iniquities I will also cause you to dwell in the cities, and the wastes shall be builded. 34 And the desolate land shall be tilled, whereas it lay desolate in the sight of all that passed by. 35 And they shall say, This land that was desolate is become like the garden of Eden; and the waste and desolate and ruined cities are become fenced, and are inhabited. 36 Then the heathen that are left round about you shall know that I the LORD build the ruined places, and plant that that was desolate: I the LORD have spoken it, and I will do it. 37 Thus saith the Lord GOD; I will yet for this be enquired of by the house of Israel, to do it for them; I will increase them with men like a flock. 38 As the holy flock, as the flock of Jerusalem in her solemn feasts; so shall the waste cities be filled with flocks of men: and they shall know that I am the LORD."*

Come While The Door Is Still Open For The Gentiles

In Matthew 22 Jesus spoke a parable of the marriage dinner. In Matthew 22:1-14 it says *"1 And Jesus answered and spake unto them again by parables, and said, 2 The kingdom of heaven is like unto a certain king, which made a marriage for his son, 3 And sent forth his servants to call them that were bidden to the wedding: and they would not come. 4 Again, he sent forth other servants, saying, Tell them which are bidden, Behold, I have prepared my dinner: my oxen and my fatlings are killed, and all things are ready: come unto the marriage. 5 But they made light of it, and went their ways, one to his farm, another to his merchandise: 6 And the remnant took his servants, and entreated them spitefully, and slew them. 7 But when the king heard thereof, he was wroth: and he sent forth his armies, and destroyed those murderers, and burned up their city. 8 Then saith he to his servants, The wedding is ready, but they which were bidden were not worthy. 9 Go ye therefore into the highways, and as many as ye shall find, bid to the marriage. 10 So those servants went out into the highways, and gathered together all as many as they found, both bad and good: and the wedding was furnished with guests. 11 And when the king came in to see the guests, he saw there a man which had not on a wedding garment: 12 And he saith unto him, Friend, how camest thou in hither not having a wedding garment? And he was speechless. 13 Then said the king to the servants, Bind him hand and foot, and take him away, and cast him into outer darkness; there shall be weeping and gnashing of teeth. 14 For many are called, but few are chosen."* Jesus Christ is calling those who are not born again to repent and accept him into their heart. If this message has convicted you then pray this prayer out loud to receive Jesus Christ in your heart:

Prayer Of Salvation

Dear Lord Jesus,
I come to you as a sinner,
I know I can't make it on my own.
Forgive me for my sins,
Come into my heart,
Come into my life.
According to your Word,
In Romans 10:9-10,
You said,
That if thou shalt confess
With thy mouth the Lord Jesus,
And shalt believe in thine heart
That God hath raised Him from the dead,
Thou shalt be saved.
For with the heart,
Man believeth unto righteousness,
And with the mouth,
Confession is made unto salvation.
Thank you Lord for saving me!
I am a new creature now.
I will pray,
I will read my Bible,
I will do the things according to your Word.
In Jesus name, Amen.

We will continue to share more about the next steps for a Christian in Chapter 10 "What Can A Christian Do?"

CHAPTER 4

Destruction For America

If when he seeth the sword come upon the land, he blow the trumpet, and warn the people; Then whosoever heareth the sound of the trumpet, and taketh not warning; if the sword come, and take him away, his blood shall be upon his own head.
Ezekiel 33:3-4

The LORD gave me the message "Destruction For America" in 1994. I preached it on 5/1/94 and sent tapes of this message all over the United States to different Christian television stations, ministries, churches and individual Christians warning them about what God is going to do to this country.

Destruction Comes When The People Of God Turn From Following God To Following Men

I Samuel 8:1-8 shows us that the prophet Samuel was old and his sons walked not in his ways and the children of Israel wanted a king like all the other nations. In I Samuel 8:1-8 it states *"1 And it came to pass, when Samuel was old, that he made his sons judges over Israel. 2 Now the name of his firstborn was Joel; and the name of his second, Abiah: they were judges in Beer-sheba. 3 And his sons walked not in his ways, but turned aside after lucre, and took bribes, and perverted judgement. 4 Then all the elders of Israel gathered themselves together, and came to Samuel unto Ramah, 5 And said unto him, Behold thou art old, and thy sons walk not in thy ways: now make us a king to judge us like all the nations. 6 But the thing displeased Samuel, when they said, Give us a king to judge us. And Samuel prayed unto the Lord. 7 And the Lord said unto Samuel, Hearken unto the voice of the people in all that they say unto thee: for they have not rejected thee, but they have rejected me, that I should not reign over them. 8 According to all the works which they have done since the day that I brought them up out of Egypt even unto this day, wherewith they have forsaken me, and served other gods, so do they also unto thee."* As Solomon said in Ecclesiastes 1:9 *" 9 The thing that hath been, it is that which shall be; and that which is done is that which shall be done: and there is no new thing under the sun."* We can see from I Samuel 8:1-8 that in the days of the prophet Samuel the children of Israel wanted to be like all the other nations and have a king over them instead of God. In the United States, many ministers tell Christians to run to the polls to vote for the next president. But we can see that God has allowed the most evil president we have ever had in this country to be elected not once but twice.

Destruction Comes When Sodomy Is Accepted In A Nation

In the United States today, the homosexuals and lesbians are perverting this whole nation through the leaders in this nation. In Genesis 19:1-14, God's Word shows us the state of Sodom and Gomorrah before He had to destroy it. In Genesis 19:1-14 it says *"1 And there came two angels to Sodom at even; and Lot sat in the gate of Sodom: and Lot seeing them rose up to meet them; and he bowed himself with his face toward the ground; 2 And he said, Behold now, my lords, turn in, I pray you, into your servant's house, and tarry all night, and wash your feet, and ye shall rise up early, and go on your ways. And they said, Nay; but we will abide in the street all night. 3 And he pressed upon them greatly; and they turned in unto him, and entered into his house; and he made them a feast, and did bake unleavened bread, and they did eat. 4 But before they lay down, the men of the city, even the men of Sodom, compassed the house round, both old and young, all the people from every quarter: 5 And they called unto Lot, and said unto him, Where are the men which came in to thee this night? bring them out unto us, that we may know them. 6 And Lot went out at the door unto them, and shut the door after him, 7 And said, I pray you, brethren, do not so wickedly. 8 Behold now, I have two daughters which have not known man; let me, I pray you, bring them out unto you, and do ye to them as is good in your eyes: only unto these men do nothing; for therefore came they under the shadow of my roof. 9 And they said, Stand back. And they said again, This one fellow came in to sojourn, and he will needs be judge: now will we deal worse with thee, than with them. And they pressed sore upon the man, even Lot, and came near to break the door. 10 But the men put forth their hand, and pulled Lot into the house to them, and shut the door. 11 And they smote the men that were at the door of the house with blindness, both small and great: so that they wearied themselves to find the door. 12 And the men said unto Lot, Hast thou here any besides? son-in-law, and thy sons, and thy daughters, and whatsoever thou hast in the city, bring them out of this place: 13 For we will destroy this place, because the cry of them is waxen great before the face of the Lord; and the Lord hath sent us to destroy it. 14 And Lot went out, and spake unto his sons in law, which married his daughters, and said, Up, get you out of this place; for the Lord will destroy this city. But he seemed as one that mocked unto his sons in law."*

This passage of scripture shows us Lot meeting with two angels at the gate of Sodom and inviting them to his house to eat. We see that before they lay down, men surround the house of Lot and want to rape these two angels of God. After the angels supernaturally deliver Lot into his house, the angels smote the men of Sodom with blindness. Even after this the men of Sodom were trying to find the door.

When open perversion is flaunted in the face of God, He must destroy it. Notice also that when Lot talked to his sons in law about Sodom and Gomorrah being destroyed that they mocked him. Similarly many have not received this message concerning the destruction for America. God not only said that he would destroy Sodom and Gomorrah but also any nation who accepts this perversion. In II Peter 2:6 it states *"6 And turning the cities of Sodom and Gomorrha into ashes condemned them with an overthrow, making them an example unto those that after should live ungodly."* Also, in Jude 1:7 *"Even as Sodom and Gomorrha, and the cities about them in like manner, giving themselves over to fornication, and going after strange flesh, are set forth for an example, suffering the vengeance of eternal fire."* These two scriptures clearly show that Sodom and Gomorrah are examples of what will happen in the future to any city, nation or people who commit the sins of homosexuality and that God will destroy them.

Pray that those bound by this demon of perversion would be delivered through salvation in Jesus Christ and be filled with the Holy Ghost.

The Signs of God's Judgement Before Destruction

There are signs that show a nation is about to be destroyed by God. We can look through the scriptures to see these signs. By observing what happened to nations before God destroyed them, we can see that America is on the road to destruction.

Violence

In Genesis 6:5-8,11-13 God's word shows us the state of the earth before He destroyed it. It says *"5 And God saw that the wickedness of man was great in the earth, and that every imagination of the thoughts of his heart was only evil continually. 6 And it repented the Lord that he had made man on the earth, and it grieved him at his heart. 7 And the Lord said, I will destroy man whom I have created from the face of the earth; both man, and beast, and the creeping thing, and the fowls of the air; for it repenteth me that I have made them. 8 But Noah found grace in the eyes of the Lord....11 The earth also was corrupt before God, and the earth was filled with violence. 12 And God looked upon the earth, and, behold, it was corrupt; for all flesh had corrupted his way upon the earth. 13 And God said unto Noah, The end of all flesh is come before me; for the earth is filled with violence through them; and, behold, I will destroy them with the earth."* Notice verse 5 says *"and that every imagination of the thoughts of his heart was only evil continually."* and verse 11 says *"the earth was filled with violence."* Compare this to America. We can see that the evil in this nation is as it was in the days of Noah. You think you have heard the worst act of violence, but then comes another incident which is more violent than the previous one.

Defeat In Battle By A Smaller Nation

The book of Joshua shows how God delivered Jericho into the hands of the children of Israel. But it also shows that after this great victory the children of Israel went to little Ai and were defeated because someone had sinned and had taken of the accursed thing. This person had put the accursed thing among their own stuff and as a result the children of Israel were accursed and could not stand before their enemies.

In Joshua 7:1-12 it says *"1 But the children of Israel committed a trespass in the accursed thing: for Achan, the son of Carmi, the son of Zabdi, the son of Zerah, of the tribe of Judah , took of the accursed thing: and the anger of the Lord was kindled against the children of Israel. 2 And Joshua sent men from Jericho to Ai, which is beside Bethaven, on the east side of Bethel, and spake unto them, saying, Go up and view the country. And the men went up and viewed Ai. 3 And they returned to Joshua, and said unto him, Let not all the people go up; but let about two or three thousand man go up and smite Ai; and make not all the people to labour thither; for they are but few. 4 So there went up thither of the people about three thousand men: and they fled before the men of Ai. 5 And the men of Ai smote of them about thirty and six men: for they chased them from before the gate even unto Shebarim, and smote them in the going down: wherefore the hearts of the people melted, and became as water. 6 And Joshua rent his clothes, and fell to the earth upon his face before the ark of the Lord until the eventide, he and the elders of Israel, and put dust upon their heads. 7 And Joshua said, Alas, O Lord God, wherefore hast thou at all brought this people over Jordan, to deliver us into the hand of the Amorites, to destroy us? would to God we had been content, and dwelt on the other side Jordan! 8 O Lord, what shall I say, when Israel turneth their backs before their enemies! 9 For the Canaanites and all the inhabitants of the land shall hear of it, and shall environ us round, and cut off our name from the earth: and what wilt thou do unto thy great name? 10 And the Lord said unto Joshua, Get thee up; wherefore liest thou thus upon thy face? 11 Israel hath sinned, and they have also transgressed my covenant which I commanded them: for they have even taken of the accursed thing, and have also stolen, and dissembled also, and they have put it even among their own stuff. 12 Therefore the children of Israel could not stand before their enemies, but turned their backs before their enemies, because they were accursed: neither will I be with you any more, except ye destroy the accursed from among you."*

We have seen through history how America has destroyed Iraq and other nations. More recently America has established itself as the only super power left on earth. But America went to a small city in Somalia and was driven out of this little nation by a small group of rebels.

Immoral Leaders

Ahab was the most evil king of his day. Similarly, President Clinton would have to be considered the most evil president in U.S. history.

In I Kings 16:29-33 it says *"29 And in the thirty and eighth year of Asa king of Judah began Ahab the son of Omri to reign over Israel: And Ahab the son of Omri reigned over Israel in Samaria twenty and two years. 30 And Ahab the son of Omri did evil in the sight of the Lord above all that were before him. 31 And it came to pass, as if it had been a light thing for him to walk in the sins of Jeroboam the son of Nebat, that he took to wife Jezebel the daughter of Ethbaal king of the Zidonians, and went and served Baal, and worshipped him. 32 And he reared up an altar for Baal in the house of Baal, which he had built in Samaria. 33 And Ahab made a grove; and Ahab did more to provoke the Lord God of Israel to anger than all the kings of Israel that were before him."* Just as Ahab and Jezebel were to Israel so are President Clinton and Hillary to the United States of America.

God's Warnings Ignored

Jeremiah, Jonah, Nahum and other prophets spoke against the sin of the people and what the consequences would be if they failed to repent. In Jeremiah 25:1-7 it says *"1 The word that came to Jeremiah concerning all the people of Judah in the fourth year of Jehoiakim the son of Josiah king of Judah, that was the first year of Nebuchadrezzar king of Babylon; 2 The which Jeremiah the prophet spake unto all the people of Judah, and to all the inhabitants of Jerusalem, saying, 3 From the thirteenth year of Josiah the son of Amon king of Judah, even unto this day, that is the three and twentieth year, the word of the LORD hath come unto me, and I have spoken unto you, rising early and speaking; but ye have not hearkened. 4 And the LORD hath sent unto you all his servants the prophets, rising early and sending them; but ye have not hearkened, nor inclined your ear to hear. 5 They said, Turn ye again now every one from his evil way, and from the evil of your doings, and dwell in the land that the LORD hath given unto you and to your fathers for ever and ever: 6 And go not after other gods to serve them, and to worship them, and provoke me not to anger with the works of your hands; and I will do you no hurt. 7 Yet ye have not hearkened unto me, saith the LORD; that ye might provoke me to anger with the works of your hands to your own hurt."* The people of Judah didn't listen and God allowed them to be in captivity for seventy years under the nation of Babylon.

In the book of Jonah, Jonah preached that in forty days, Nineveh would be overthrown As a result the people of Nineveh repented. In Jonah 3:1-10 it says

"1 And the word of the LORD came unto Jonah the second time, saying, 2 Arise, go unto Nineveh, that great city, and preach unto it the preaching that I bid thee. 3 So Jonah arose, and went unto Nineveh, according to the word of the LORD. Now

Nineveh was an exceeding great city of three days' journey. 4 And Jonah began to enter into the city a day's journey, and he cried, and said, Yet forty days, and Nineveh shall be overthrown. 5 So the people of Nineveh believed God, and proclaimed a fast, and put on sackcloth, from the greatest of them even to the least of them. 6 For word came unto the king of Nineveh, and he arose from his throne, and he laid his robe from him, and covered him with sackcloth, and sat in ashes. 7 And he caused it to be proclaimed and published through Nineveh by the decree of the king and his nobles, saying, Let neither man nor beast, herd nor flock, taste any thing: let them not feed, nor drink water: 8 But let man and beast be covered with sackcloth, and cry mightily unto God: yea, let them turn every one from his evil way, and from the violence that is in their hands. 9 Who can tell if God will turn and repent, and turn away from his fierce anger, that we perish not? 10 And God saw their works, that they turned from their evil way; and God repented of the evil, that he had said that he would do unto them; and he did it not."

Several years later Nineveh turned wicked again and God spoke of their destruction through the prophet Nahum. Nahum 3:1-7 shows the state of Nineveh before God destroyed it. It says

"1 Woe to the bloody city! it is all full of lies and robbery; the prey departeth not; 2 The noise of a whip, and the noise of the rattling of the wheels, and of the prancing horses, and of the jumping chariots. 3 The horseman lifteth up both the bright sword and the glittering spear: and there is a multitude of slain, and a great number of carcases; and there is none end of their corpses; they stumble upon their corpses: 4 Because of the multitude of the whoredoms of the wellfavoured harlot, the mistress of witchcrafts, that selleth nations through her whoredoms, and families through her witchcrafts. 5 Behold, I am against thee, saith the LORD of hosts; and I will discover thy skirts upon thy face, and I will shew the nations thy

nakedness, and the kingdoms thy shame. 6 And I will cast abominable filth upon thee, and make thee vile, and will set thee as a gazingstock. 7 And it shall come to pass, that all they that look upon thee shall flee from thee, and say, Nineveh is laid waste: who will bemoan her? whence shall I seek comforters for thee?"

Just as in the past, God's warnings are being ignored today. In the Pacific Northwest, a widely distributed Christian newspaper recently cancelled prophetic articles which were being printed in their paper because it "offended" some churches.   These prophetic articles were being written by a man of God who has prophesied God's warnings to leaders around the world, and those prophecies have come to pass.

We can see that because of their sins, God had to destroy Judah and Nineveh.   There should be no question in our minds that God must destroy America.

Idolatry

Look at the idolatry in our country today. In Colossians 3:5-6 it says *"5 Mortify therefore your members which are upon the earth; fornication, uncleanness, inordinate affection, evil concupiscence, and covetousness, which is idolatry: 6 For which things' sake the wrath of God cometh on the children of disobedience:"*   The word inordinate means "excessive." The word concupiscence means "evil desire or indwelling sin." The word covetousness means "the wish to have more."[1] Colossians shows us that these things are idolatry (see the end of verse 5).

Many Ministers Turn From The Truth To Fables Or Doctrines Of Men

Notice what Paul says about ministers who turned from the truth. In Philippians 3:17-19 it says *"17 Brethren, be followers together of me, and mark them which walk so as ye have us for an example. 18 (For many walk, of whom I have told you often, and now tell you even weeping, that they are the enemies of the cross of Christ: 19 Whose end is destruction, whose God is their belly, and whose glory is in their shame, who mind earthly things.)* The earthly messages today have perverted the minds of God's people.

Many have believed the lie that gain is godliness but notice what the apostle Paul said in I Timothy 6:3-7. It says *"3 If any man teach otherwise, and consent not to wholesome words, even the words of our Lord Jesus Christ, and to the doctrine which is according to godliness; 4 He is proud, knowing nothing, but doting about questions and strifes of words, whereof cometh envy, strife, railings, evil surmisings, 5 Perverse disputings of men of corrupt minds, and destitute of the truth, supposing that gain is godliness: from such withdraw thyself. 6 But godliness with contentment is great gain. 7 For we brought nothing into this world, and it is certain we can carry nothing out."* In many churches the gospel of gain and greed are preached and people are running to hear these lies of the devil. But Paul said in the last part of verse 5 *"from such withdraw thyself."* The Bible says the exact opposite of what these false teachers are teaching today. In II Timothy 4:1-4 it says *" 1 I charge thee therefore before God, and the Lord Jesus Christ, who shall judge the quick and the dead at his appearing and his kingdom; 2 Preach the word; be instant in season, out of season; reprove, rebuke, exhort with all longsuffering and doctrine. 3 For the time will come when they will not endure sound doctrine; but after their own lusts shall they heap to themselves teachers, having itching ears; 4 And they shall turn away their ears from the truth, and shall be turned unto fables."* The apostle Paul tells of a time when the people will not endure sound doctrine but after their own lusts shall they heap to themselves teachers, having itching ears and how they will turn their ears from the truth unto fables. We are living in this day now. People in many of the churches today don't want to know what the Bible says. Instead they listen to false teachers preaching things that are not in the Bible. We must pray that as many as can will repent and that all pastors will preach the truth of God's Holy Word.

A False Peace

Notice the false peace in our nation today. The prophet Jeremiah spoke about a false peace in his day. In Jeremiah 14:13-16 it says *"13 Then said I, Ah, Lord GOD! behold, the prophets say unto them, Ye shall not see the sword, neither shall ye have famine; but I will give you assured peace in this place. 14 Then the LORD said unto me, The prophets prophesy lies in my name: I sent them not, neither have I commanded them, neither spake unto them: they prophesy unto you a false vision and divination, and a thing of nought, and the deceit of their heart. 15 Therefore thus saith the LORD concerning the prophets that prophesy in my name, and I sent them not, yet they say, Sword and famine shall not be in this land; By sword and famine shall those prophets be consumed. 16 And the people to whom they prophesy shall be cast out in the streets of Jerusalem because of the famine and the sword; and they shall have none to bury them, them, their wives, nor their sons, nor their daughters: for I will pour their wickedness upon them."* The apostle Paul said in I Thessalonians 5:3 *"3 For when they shall say, Peace and safety; then sudden destruction cometh upon them, as travail upon a woman with child; and they shall not escape."* The world is more explosive than ever. But our nation is demilitarizing: we are shutting down bases, laying off multitudes in our military and our enemies are building up.

Here is a quote from a newspaper article titled "Security Lax At Nuke Labs: Background Checks On Foreign Visitors Were Stopped In 1994". In the article it states "After President Clinton took office, the Energy Department allowed two of its most sensitive nuclear weapons labs to halt background checks on foreign guests to cope with soaring numbers of visiting Chinese and Russian scientists. Officials now concede the move was a security blunder. While direct evidence has not emerged of espionage by the visitors, congressional investigators found at least 13 scientists with suspected foreign intelligence ties were allowed into the labs without proper CIA or FBI scrutiny.....Security checks, mandatory before 1994, were reinstated last November amid growing Clinton administration worries about Chinese espionage at the government's premier weapons labs. U.S. officials don't know if nuclear secrets were lost to any of the 4,409 Russian and Chinese visitors between 1994 and late 1998, when checks were reinstated." Our reprobate President allowed 4,409 people from the two greatest enemies of our nation (Russia and China) to steal our nuclear secrets. If you are still doubting that God is about to destroy this country, I pray that the spirit of blindness be broken off of you so you can draw closer to Jesus while there is still time.

In I Kings chapter 22 king Ahab asked the false prophets of Israel if he should fight Syria in Ramoth-gilead. By following their answer king Ahab lost his life. In I Kings 22:1-8 it says *"1 And they continued three years without war between Syria and Israel. 2 And it came to pass in the third year, that Jehoshaphat the king of Judah came down to the king of Israel. 3 And the king of Israel said unto his servants, Know ye that Ramoth in Gilead is ours, and we be still, and take it not out of the hand of the king of Syria? 4 And he said unto Jehoshaphat, Wilt thou go with me to battle to Ramoth-gilead? And Jehoshaphat said to the king of Israel, I am as thou art, my people as thy people, my horses as thy horses. 5 And Jehoshaphat said unto the king of Israel, Inquire, I pray thee, at the word of the LORD to day. 6 Then the king of Israel gathered the prophets together, about four hundred men, and said unto them, Shall I go against Ramoth-gilead to battle, or shall I forbear? And they said, Go up; for the Lord shall deliver it into the hand of the king. 7 And Jehoshaphat said, Is there not here a prophet of the LORD besides, that we might inquire of him? 8 And the king of Israel said unto Jehoshaphat, There is yet one man, Micaiah the son of Imlah, by whom we may inquire of the LORD: but I hate him; for he doth not prophesy good concerning me, but evil. And Jehoshaphat said, Let not the king say so."*

Jehoshaphat knew that the four hundred prophets were not speaking a word from the Lord. He asked king Ahab for a prophet of the Lord to inquire of him. This prophet's name was Micaiah. King Ahab hated Micaiah because he always prophesied evil concerning him. In I Kings 22:14-18 it says *"14 And Micaiah said, As the LORD liveth, what the LORD saith unto me, that will I speak. 15 So he came to the king. And the king said unto him, Micaiah, shall we go against Ramoth-gilead to battle, or shall we forbear? And he answered him, Go, and prosper: for the LORD shall deliver it into the hand of the king. 16 And the king said unto him, How many times shall I adjure thee that thou tell me nothing but that which is true in the name of the LORD? 17 And he said, I saw all Israel scattered upon the hills, as sheep that have not a shepherd: and the LORD said, These have no master: let them return every man to his house in peace. 18 And the king of Israel said unto Jehoshaphat, Did I not tell thee that he would prophesy no good concerning me, but evil?"* In I Kings 22:6 it shows how God allowed a lying spirit to speak through the prophets of

Israel. King Ahab believed these false prophets over the true prophet Micaiah and as a result king Ahab died in the battle. In Kings 22:29-40 it says

"29 So the king of Israel and Jehoshaphat the king of Judah went up to Ramoth-gilead. 30 And the king of Israel said unto Jehoshaphat, I will disguise myself, and enter into the battle; but put thou on thy robes. And the king of Israel disguised himself, and went into the battle. 31 But the king of Syria commanded his thirty and two captains that had rule over his chariots, saying, Fight neither with small nor great, save only with the king of Israel. 32 And it came to pass, when the captains of the chariots saw Jehoshaphat, that they said, Surely it is the king of Israel. And they turned aside to fight against him: and Jehoshaphat cried out. 33 And it came to pass, when the captains of the chariots perceived that it was not the king of Israel, that they turned back from pursuing him. 34 And a certain man drew a bow at a venture, and smote the king of Israel between the joints of the harness: wherefore he said unto the driver of his chariot, Turn thine hand, and carry me out of the host; for I am wounded. 35 And the battle increased that day: and the king was stayed up in his chariot against the Syrians, and died at even: and the blood ran out of the wound into the midst of the chariot. 36 And there went a proclamation throughout the host about the going down of the sun, saying, Every man to his city, and every man to his own country. 37 So the king died, and was brought to Samaria; and they buried the king in Samaria. 38 And one washed the chariot in the pool of Samaria; and the dogs licked up his blood; and they washed his armour; according unto the word of the LORD which he spake. 39 Now the rest of the acts of Ahab, and all that he did, and the ivory house which he made, and all the cities that he built, are they not written in the book of the chronicles of the kings of Israel? 40 So Ahab slept with his fathers; and Ahaziah his son reigned in his stead.

When A Nation Turns From God , He Uses Another Nation To Destroy It

When the people of Judah refused to repent of their evil ways, the prophet Jeremiah prophesied that they would be invaded by Babylon. In Jeremiah 25:1-14 it says *"1 The word that came to Jeremiah concerning all the people of Judah in the fourth year of Jehoiakim the son of Josiah king of Judah, that was the first year of Nebuchadrezzar king of Babylon; 2 The which Jeremiah the prophet spake unto all the people of Judah, and to all the inhabitants of Jerusalem, saying, 3 From the thirteenth year of Josiah the son of Amon king of Judah, even unto this day, that is the three and twentieth year, the word of the LORD hath come unto me, and I have spoken unto you, rising early and speaking; but ye have not hearkened. 4 And the LORD hath sent unto you all his servants the prophets, rising early and sending them; but ye have not hearkened, nor inclined your ear to hear. 5 They said, Turn ye again now every one from his evil way, and from the evil of your doings, and dwell in the land that the LORD hath given unto you and to your fathers for ever and ever: 6 And go not after other gods to serve them, and to worship them, and provoke me not to anger with the works of your hands; and I will do you no hurt. 7 Yet ye have not hearkened unto me, saith the LORD; that ye might provoke me to anger with the works of your hands to your own hurt. 8 Therefore thus saith the LORD of hosts; Because ye have not heard my words, 9 Behold, I will send and take all the families of the north, saith the LORD, and Nebuchadrezzar the king of Babylon, my servant, and will bring them against this land, and against the inhabitants thereof, and against all these nations round about, and will utterly destroy them, and make them an astonishment, and an hissing, and perpetual desolations. 10 Moreover I will take from them the voice of mirth, and the voice of gladness, the voice of the bridegroom, and the voice of the bride, the sound of the millstones, and the light of the candle. 11 And this whole land shall be a desolation, and an astonishment; and these nations shall serve the king of Babylon seventy years. 12 And it shall come to pass, when seventy years are accomplished, that I will punish the king of Babylon, and that nation, saith the LORD, for their iniquity, and the land of the Chaldeans, and will make it perpetual desolations. 13 And I will bring upon that land all my words which I have pronounced against it, even all that is written in this book, which Jeremiah hath prophesied against all the nations. 14 For many nations and great kings shall serve themselves of them also: and I will recompense them according to their deeds, and according to the works of their own hands."* God allowed the people of Judah to be in bondage to Babylon for 70 years.

After the seventy years God allowed Media-Persia to overthrow Babylon as the prophet Jeremiah spoke in Jeremiah 25:12. In Daniel 5:1-9, 24-31 it says *"1 Belshazzar the king made a great feast to a thousand of his lords, and drank wine before the thousand. 2 Belshazzar, whiles he tasted the wine, commanded to bring the golden and silver vessels which his father Nebuchadnezzar had taken out of the temple which was in Jerusalem; that the king, and his princes, his wives, and his concubines, might drink therein. 3 Then they brought the golden vessels that were taken out of the temple of the house of God which was at Jerusalem; and the king, and his princes, his wives, and his concubines, drank in them. 4 They drank wine, and praised the gods of gold, and of silver, of brass, of iron, of wood, and of stone. 5 In the same hour came forth fingers of a man's hand, and wrote over against the candlestick upon the plaster of the wall of the king's palace: and the king saw the part of the hand that wrote. 6 Then the king's countenance was changed, and his thoughts troubled him, so that the joints of his loins were loosed, and his knees smote one against another.*

7 The king cried aloud to bring in the astrologers, the Chaldeans, and the soothsayers. And the king spake, and said to the wise men of Babylon, Whosoever shall read this writing, and shew me the interpretation thereof, shall be clothed with scarlet, and have a chain of gold about his neck, and shall be the third ruler in the kingdom. 8 Then came in all the king's wise men: but they could not read the writing, nor make known to the king the interpretation thereof. 9 Then was king Belshazzar greatly troubled, and his countenance was changed in him, and his lords were astonied. 24 Then was the part of the hand sent from him; and this writing was written. 25 And this is the writing that was written, MENE, MENE, TEKEL, UPHARSIN. 26 This is the interpretation of the thing: MENE; God hath numbered thy kingdom, and finished it. 27 TEKEL; Thou art weighed in the balances, and art found wanting. 28 PERES; Thy kingdom is divided, and given to the Medes and Persians. 29 Then commanded Belshazzar, and they clothed Daniel with scarlet, and put a chain of gold about his neck, and made a proclamation concerning him, that he should be the third ruler in the kingdom. 30 In that night was Belshazzar the king of the Chaldeans slain. 31 And Darius the Median took the kingdom, being about threescore and two years old."

In Deuteronomy God showed how specific curses would come on a disobedient nation. Deuteronomy 28:47-52 says "*47 Because thou servedst not the LORD thy God with joyfulness, and with gladness of heart, for the abundance of all things; 48 Therefore shalt thou serve thine enemies which the LORD shall send against thee, in hunger, and in thirst, and in nakedness, and in want of all things: and he shall put a yoke of iron upon thy neck, until he have destroyed thee. 49 The LORD shall bring a nation against thee from far, from the end of the earth, as swift as the eagle flieth; a nation whose tongue thou shalt not understand; 50 A nation of fierce countenance, which shall not regard the person of the old, nor shew favour to the young:*

51 And he shall eat the fruit of thy cattle, and the fruit of thy land, until thou be destroyed: which also shall not leave thee either corn, wine, or oil, or the increase of thy kine, or flocks of thy sheep, until he have destroyed thee. 52 And he shall besiege thee in all thy gates, until thy high and fenced walls come down, wherein thou trustedst, throughout all thy land: and he shall besiege thee in all thy gates throughout all thy land, which the LORD thy God hath given thee." Notice that in verse 49 God said *"The LORD shall bring a nation against thee from far, from the end of the earth, as swift as the eagle flieth; a nation whose tongue thou shalt not understand."*

Just as God used the evil king Nebuchadrezzar against the people of Judah, God will use Russia and the evil countries formerly called the U.S.S.R. against the United States of America. A recent newspaper article was titled "Exercise By Russian Bombers Alert U.S." In the article it stated " Two Russian strategic bombers flew within striking distance of the United States last week as part of Moscow's largest military exercises since the end of the Cold War, astounding U.S. officials and underlining recent Western concerns about the military leadership in Moscow. The TU-95 Bear bombers were intercepted by four U.S. F-15 fighters and a P-3 patrol plane near Iceland early Friday morning and escorted in a clockwise flight around the island, U.S. officials said. Norway, which like Iceland is a NATO member, also scrambled jets to meet two other TU-140 Blackjack bombers that flew down the Norwegian coastline, but Russian reports said the interceptors failed to reach the bombers before they turned back.... Although Russian bombers often probed Western defenses during the Cold War, officials said no such activity had been recorded in a decade, and the appearance of the Russian long-range bombers over Iceland and Norway surprised NATO....They want to show us they aren't afraid, that they too have missiles and that they consider NATO's out-of theater actions their main military threat, said Stephen J. Blank, a Russian expert at the U.S. Army War College who returned from a trip to Moscow 10 days ago. The bomber flights occurred five days into what Russia said was a previously scheduled exercise, West '99, that involved up to 50,000 troops from five military districts and three naval fleets". Again we see the blindness of our leaders in America. With the United States having no defense system to protect itself it is just a matter of time until Russia and the former countries of the U.S.S.R. will invade this country.

Remember Lot

In Genesis 19 Lot was totally unaware that God was about to destroy Sodom and Gomorrha. Today many in America are the same way, they are so caught up in the things going on in this nation that they are unaware that God will soon destroy this country. In II Peter 2:6-9 it says *"6 And turning the cities of Sodom and Gomorrha into ashes condemned them with an overthrow, making them an ensample unto those that after should live ungodly; 7 And delivered just Lot, vexed with the filthy conversation of the wicked: 8 (For that righteous man dwelling among them, in seeing and hearing, vexed his righteous soul from day to day with their unlawful deeds;) 9 The Lord knoweth how to deliver the godly out of temptations, and to reserve the unjust unto the day of judgment to be punished:"* We do not want to be like Lot, unprepared for what is about to happen to this nation. We want to be like Noah.

Remember Noah

Noah was a just man who walked with God and obeyed God by building an ark to the saving of his house from the destruction of the earth. In II Peter 2:4-5 it says *"4 For if God spared not the angels that sinned, but cast them down to hell, and delivered them into chains of darkness, to be reserved unto judgment; 5 And spared not the old world, but saved Noah the eighth person, a preacher of righteousness, bringing in the flood upon the world of the ungodly;"* Also, in Hebrews 11:7 it says *"7 By faith Noah, being warned of God of things not seen as yet, moved with fear, prepared an ark to the saving of his house; by the which he condemned the world, and became heir of the righteousness which is by faith."* We must prepare spiritually and physically for what is going to happen to this nation. I will talk more about this in Chapter 10, "What Can A Christian Do?"

CHAPTER 5

What Prophecies Must Be Fulfilled Before The Return Of Jesus Christ?

"Behold, I show you a mystery; We shall not all sleep, but we shall all be changed, In a moment, in the twinkling of an eye, at the last trump; for the trumpet shall sound, and the dead shall be raised incorruptible, and we shall be changed."
I Corinthians 15:51-52

This chapter shows the major things that will come to pass before Jesus Christ returns and when He returns for His church. These may not be in order but will come to pass before the return of Jesus Christ.

God's Judgement Coming On The Church

In I Peter 4:17-18 God's word speaks about the judgement coming on the church before God will judge the world. In I Peter 4:17-18 it says *"17 For the time is come that judgment must begin at the house of God: and if it first begin at us, what shall the end be of them that obey not the gospel of God? 18 And if the righteous scarcely be saved, where shall the ungodly and the sinner appear?"* In the book of Malachi it speaks of

God purifying the sons of Levi, or the ministry, and purging them so that they can offer unto the Lord an offering in righteousness. Malachi 2:17 says *"Ye have wearied the LORD with your words. Yet ye say, Wherein have we wearied him? When ye say, Every one that doeth evil is good in the sight of the LORD, and he delighteth in them; or, Where is the God of judgment?"* And in Malachi 3:1-3 it says *"1 Behold, I will send my messenger, and he shall prepare the way before me: and the Lord, whom ye seek, shall suddenly come to his temple, even the messenger of the covenant, whom ye delight in: behold, he shall come, saith the LORD of hosts. 2 But who may abide the day of his coming? and who shall stand when he appeareth? for he is like a refiner's fire, and like fullers' soap: 3 And he shall sit as a refiner and purifier of silver: and he shall purify the sons of Levi, and purge them as gold and silver, that they may offer unto the LORD an offering in righteousness."* God will purify the ministry so that they will only glorify him. See Chapter 8 - "Why God Must Judge The Church" for important details covering this topic.

The Door Closing To The Gentiles

The Holy Bible tells us that there is coming a time when no more Gentiles can be saved and God will visit his chosen people the children of Israel. In Acts 15:14 it says *"Simeon hath declared how God at the first did visit the Gentiles, to take out of them a people for his name."* and in Romans 11:25 it says *"For I would not, brethren, that ye should be ignorant of this mystery, lest ye should be wise in your own conceits; that blindness in part is happened to Israel, until the fulness of the Gentiles be come in."* Chapter 3 - "The Door Closing To The Gentiles" covers the details of this topic.

Destruction For America

The Lord gave me a message on May 1, 1994 about why God was going to destroy America. Chapter 4, titled "Destruction For America" covers this topic in detail.

The Battle Of Magog
(The U.S.S.R. and other nations
warring against Israel)

In the book of Ezekiel chapter 38 and chapter 39, the prophet Ezekiel prophesied of a future war between Israel and the U.S.S.R. and other nations with it. In Ezekiel 38:1-23 it says *"1 And the word of the LORD came unto me, saying, 2 Son of man, set thy face against Gog, the land of Magog, the chief prince of Meshech and Tubal, and prophesy against him, 3 And say, Thus saith the Lord GOD; Behold, I am against thee, O Gog, the chief prince of Meshech and Tubal: 4 And I will turn thee back, and put hooks into thy jaws, and I will bring thee forth, and all thine army, horses and horsemen, all of them clothed with all sorts of armour, even a great company with bucklers and shields, all of them handling swords: 5 Persia, Ethiopia, and Libya with them; all of them with shield and helmet: 6 Gomer, and all his bands; the house of Togarmah of the north quarters, and all his bands: and many people with thee. 7 Be thou prepared, and prepare for thyself, thou, and all thy company that are assembled unto thee, and be thou a guard unto them. 8 After many days thou shalt be visited: in the latter years thou shalt come into the land that is brought back from the sword, and is gathered out of many people, against the mountains of Israel, which have been always waste: but it is brought forth out of the nations, and they shall dwell safely all of them. 9 Thou shalt ascend and come like a storm, thou shalt be like a cloud to cover the land, thou, and all thy bands, and many people with thee. 10 Thus saith the Lord GOD; It shall also come to pass, that at the same time shall things come into thy mind, and thou shalt think an evil thought: 11 And thou shalt say, I will go up to the land of unwalled villages; I will go to them that are at rest, that dwell safely, all of them dwelling without walls, and having neither bars nor gates, 12 To take a spoil, and to take a prey; to turn thine hand upon the desolate places that are now inhabited, and upon the people that are gathered out of the nations, which have gotten cattle and goods, that dwell in the midst of the land. 13 Sheba, and Dedan, and the merchants of Tarshish, with all the young lions thereof, shall say unto thee, Art thou come to take a spoil? hast thou gathered thy company to take a prey? to carry away silver and gold, to take away cattle and goods, to take a great spoil? 14 Therefore, son of man, prophesy and say unto Gog, Thus saith the Lord GOD; In that day when my people of Israel dwelleth safely, shalt thou not know it? 15 And thou shalt come from thy place out of the north parts, thou, and many people with thee, all of them riding upon horses, a great company, and a mighty army: 16 And thou shalt come up against my people of Israel, as a cloud to cover the land; it shall be in the latter days, and I will bring thee against my land, that the heathen may know me, when I shall be sanctified in thee, O Gog, before their eyes. 17 Thus saith the Lord GOD; Art thou he of whom I have spoken in old time by my servants the prophets of Israel, which prophesied in those days many years that I would bring thee against them? 18 And it shall come to pass at the same time when Gog shall come against the land of Israel, saith the Lord GOD, that my fury shall come up in my face. 19 For in my jealousy and in the fire of my wrath have I spoken, Surely in that day there shall be a great shaking in the land of Israel; 20 So that the fishes of the sea, and the fowls of the heaven, and the beasts of the field, and all creeping things that creep upon the earth, and all the men that are upon the face of the earth, shall shake at my presence, and the mountains shall be thrown down, and the steep places shall fall, and every wall shall fall to the ground. 21 And I will call for a sword against him throughout all my mountains, saith the Lord GOD: every man's sword shall be against his brother. 22 And I will plead against him with pestilence and with blood; and I will rain upon him, and upon his bands, and upon the many people that are with him, an overflowing rain, and great hailstones, fire, and brimstone. 23 Thus will I magnify myself, and sanctify myself; and I will be known in the eyes of many nations, and they shall know that I am the LORD."*

To find out who the nations in this passage are today, I looked at a historical map titled "The Table Of Nations According To Genesis 10" (Copyright by Rand McNally & Company). I used this map to trace the descendants of Shem , Ham and Japheth and was able to find the geographical location of each nation spoken of in Ezekiel. I then compared the locations of these places on this historical map to the same locations today to figure out the modern name for each nation.

Based on this map study, one can look at Ezekiel chapter 38 and determine who these modern nations are that come against Israel. In Ezekiel 38:2 it says *" Son of man, set thy face against Gog, the land of Magog, the chief prince of Meshech and Tubal, and prophesy against him,"* From the maps, the land of Magog is a part of the U.S.S.R. and Gog is the leader of the U.S.S.R. Meshech and Tubal are modern day Turkey. The leader of the U.S.S.R. will be over Turkey which has not happened just yet. Today the nation of Turkey is a friend of Israel but this will change in the future to fulfill this prophecy. I am still using the term U.S.S.R. The former countries of the U.S.S.R. no longer go by this term and have deceived our nation to think that they have changed, but they have not changed at all. Notice in Ezekiel 38:4 that God puts a hook in the jaw of the leader of the U.S.S.R. In Ezekiel 38:4 it says *"And I will turn thee back, and put hooks into thy jaws, and I will bring thee forth, and all thine army, horses and horsemen, all of them clothed with all sorts of armour, even a great company with bucklers and shields, all of them handling swords:"* The prophet Ezekiel prophesied of the weapons of war used in his day. In today's modern wars they use tanks, missiles, airplanes and other modern equipment.

In Ezekiel 38:5-6 it says *"5 Persia, Ethiopia, and Libya with them; all of them with shield and helmet: 6 Gomer, and all his bands; the house of Togarmah of the north quarters, and all his bands: and many people with thee."* From the maps, Persia is modern day Iran, Ethiopia is the same Ethiopia and Libya is the same Libya. Gomer and his bands are part of the U.S.S.R., the house of Togarmah of the north quarters is a small part of Turkey and a part of the U.S.S.R.

In Ezekiel 38:8 it says *"After many days thou shalt be visited: in the latter years thou shalt come into the land that is brought back from the sword, and is gathered out of many people, against the mountains of Israel, which have been always waste: but it is brought forth out of the nations, and they shall dwell safely all of them."* Notice the scripture says" *the latter years"* which is the time we are living in today. From it's destruction in 70 A.D. to it's formation as a nation in May 1948 the nation of Israel did not exist. But God's Word was fulfilled when Israel became a nation.

In Ezekiel 38:13 it says *"Sheba, and Dedan, and the merchants of Tarshish, with all the young lions thereof, shall say unto thee, Art thou come to take a spoil? hast thou gathered thy company to take a prey? to carry away silver and gold, to take away cattle and goods, to take a great spoil?"* From the maps Sheba and Dedan are modern day Saudi Arabia and Tarshish is modern day Spain and Portugal. These nations are looking at Gog and the other nations trying to take a spoil from Israel.

In Ezekiel 38:15 it says *"And thou shalt come from thy place out of the north parts, thou, and many people with thee, all of them riding upon horses, a great company, and a mighty army:"* From this scripture and looking at modern maps Gog (the leader of the former nations of the U.S.S.R.) and these other nations will come through the nation of Syria.

In Ezekiel 39:1-16 it says *"1 Therefore, thou son of man, prophesy against Gog, and say, Thus saith the Lord GOD; Behold, I am against thee, O Gog, the chief prince of Meshech and Tubal: 2 And I will turn thee back, and leave but the sixth part of thee, and will cause thee to come up from the north parts, and will bring thee upon the mountains of Israel: 3 And I will smite thy bow out of thy left hand, and will cause thine arrows to fall out of thy right hand. 4 Thou shalt fall upon the mountains of Israel, thou, and all thy bands, and the people that is with thee: I will give thee unto the ravenous birds of every sort, and to the beasts of the field to be devoured. 5 Thou shalt fall upon the open field: for I have spoken it, saith the Lord GOD. 6 And I will send a fire on Magog, and among them that dwell carelessly in the isles: and they shall know that I am the LORD. 7 So will I make my holy name known in the midst of my people Israel; and I will not let them pollute my holy name any more: and the heathen shall know that I am the LORD, the Holy One in Israel. 8 Behold, it is come, and it is done, saith the Lord GOD; this is the day whereof I have spoken. 9 And they that dwell in the cities of Israel shall go forth, and shall set on fire and burn the weapons, both the shields and the bucklers, the bows and the arrows, and the handstaves, and the spears, and they shall burn them with fire seven years: 10 So that they shall take no wood out of the field, neither cut down any out of the forests; for they shall burn the weapons with fire: and they shall spoil those that spoiled them, and rob those that robbed them, saith the Lord GOD. 11 And it shall come to pass in that day, that I will give unto Gog a place there of graves in Israel, the valley of the passengers on the east of the sea: and it shall stop the noses of the passengers: and there shall they bury Gog and all his multitude: and they shall call it The valley of Hamongog. 12 And seven months shall the house of Israel be burying of them, that they may cleanse the land. 13 Yea, all the people of the land shall bury them; and it shall be to them a renown the day that I shall be glorified, saith the Lord GOD. 14 And they shall sever out men of continual employment, passing through the land to bury with the passengers those that remain upon the face of the earth, to cleanse it: after the end of seven months shall they search. 15 And the passengers that pass through the land, when any seeth a man's bone, then shall he set up a sign by it, till the buriers have buried it in the valley of Hamongog. 16 And also the name of the city shall be Hamonah. Thus shall they cleanse the land."*

In Ezekiel 39:1-16 we see how God destroys all these nations that come against Israel and leaves a sixth part of them. The Israelites shall burn the weapons seven years and will take seven months to bury them. Let's look at these three verses in Ezekiel chapter 39. They say:

Ezekiel 39: 2 "And I will turn thee back, and leave but the sixth part of thee, and will cause thee to come up from the north parts, and will bring thee upon the mountains of Israel:"

Ezekiel 39:9 "And they that dwell in the cities of Israel shall go forth, and shall set on fire and burn the weapons, both the shields and the bucklers, the bows and the arrows, and the handstaves, and the spears, and they shall burn them with fire seven years:"

Ezekiel 39:12 "And seven months shall the house of Israel be burying of them, that they may cleanse the land."

The Signs In The Heavens Before Jesus Returns

Many people say that Jesus can return at any moment. But this is not true. In Matthew 24 Jesus Christ told us about signs that must occur in the heavens before His return. In Matthew 24:29-31 it says *"29 Immediately after the tribulation of those days shall the sun be darkened, and the moon shall not give her light, and the stars shall fall from heaven, and the powers of the heavens shall be shaken: 30 And then shall appear the sign of the Son of man in heaven: and then shall all the tribes of the earth mourn, and they shall see the Son of man coming in the clouds of heaven with power and great glory. 31 And he shall send his angels with a great sound of a trumpet, and they shall gather together his elect from the four winds, from one end of heaven to the other."* Notice in verse 29 the changes in the sun, moon and stars before Jesus Christ returns. This is a very important passage because it shows that Jesus will not return at any moment. Remember Matthew 24:29-31 because it will be referred to later.

In Acts chapter 2 as Peter was preaching on the day of Pentecost he also spoke on what Jesus said. In Acts 2:17-20 it says *"17 And it shall come to pass in the last days, saith God, I will pour out of my Spirit upon all flesh: and your sons and your daughters shall prophesy, and your young men shall see visions, and your old men shall dream dreams: 18 And on my servants and on my handmaidens I will pour out in those days of my Spirit; and they shall prophesy: 19 And I will shew wonders in heaven above, and signs in the earth beneath; blood, and fire, and vapour of smoke: 20 The sun shall be turned into darkness, and the moon into blood, before that great and notable day of the Lord come: "*

Joel 2:10 and Joel 2:28-31 also speak of this key sign. In Joel 2:10, it says *"The earth shall quake before them; the heavens shall tremble: the sun and the moon shall be dark, and the stars shall withdraw their shining:* Joel 2:28-31 says *28 And it shall come to pass afterward, that I will pour out my spirit upon all flesh; and your sons and your daughters shall prophesy, your old men shall dream dreams, your young men shall see visions: 29 And also upon the servants and upon the handmaids in those days will I pour out my spirit. 30 And I will shew wonders in the heavens and in the earth, blood, and fire, and pillars of smoke. 31 The sun shall be turned into darkness, and the moon into blood, before the great and the terrible day of the LORD come."*

We also see this same sign in the book of Revelation 6:12-14 (the sixth seal) and in Revelation 8:12 (the fourth trumpet). In Revelation 6:12-14 it says *"12 And I beheld when he had opened the sixth seal, and, lo, there was a great earthquake; and the sun became black as sackcloth of hair, and the moon became as blood; 13 And the stars of heaven fell unto the earth, even as a fig tree casteth her untimely figs, when she is shaken of a mighty wind. 14 And the heaven departed as a scroll when it is rolled together; and every mountain and island were moved out of their places."* and in Revelation 8:12 it says *"12 And the fourth angel sounded, and the third part of the sun was smitten, and the third part of the moon, and the third part of the stars; so as the third part of them was darkened, and the day shone not for a third part of it, and the night likewise."*

The Opening Of The Six Seals

The scriptures above show specific signs in the heavens occurring at the sixth seal and that this happens before Jesus Christ returns. This means all six seals will be opened before the return of Jesus Christ. In Revelation chapter 6 it shows seals one through six being opened. In Revelation 6:1-17 it says *"1 And I saw when the Lamb opened one of the seals, and I heard, as it were the noise of thunder, one of the four beasts saying, Come and see. 2 And I saw, and behold a white horse: and he that sat on him had a bow; and a crown was given unto him: and he went forth conquering, and to conquer. 3 And when he had opened the second seal, I heard the second beast say, Come and see. 4 And there went out another horse that was red: and power was given to him that sat thereon to take peace from the earth, and that they should kill one another: and there was given unto him a great sword. 5 And when he had opened the third seal, I heard the third beast say, Come and see. And I beheld, and lo a black horse; and he that sat on him had a pair of balances in his hand. 6 And I heard a voice in the midst of the four beasts say, A measure of wheat for a penny, and three measures of barley for a penny; and see thou hurt not the oil and the wine. 7 And when he had opened the fourth seal, I heard the voice of the fourth beast say, Come and see. 8 And I looked, and behold a pale horse: and his name that sat on him was Death, and Hell followed with him. And power was given unto them over the fourth part of the earth, to kill with sword, and with hunger, and with death, and with the beasts of the earth. 9 And when he had opened the fifth seal, I saw under the altar the souls of them that were slain for the word of God, and for the testimony which they held: 10 And they cried with a loud voice, saying, How long, O Lord, holy and true, dost thou not judge and avenge our blood on them that dwell on the earth? 11 And white robes were given unto every one of them; and it was said unto them, that they should rest yet for a little season, until their fellowservants also and their brethren, that should be killed as they were, should be fulfilled. 12 And I beheld when he had opened the sixth seal, and, lo, there was a great earthquake; and the sun became black as sackcloth of hair, and the moon became as blood; 13 And the stars of heaven fell unto the earth, even as a fig tree casteth her untimely figs, when she is shaken of a mighty wind. 14 And the heaven departed as a scroll when it is rolled together; and every mountain and island were moved out of their places. 15 And the kings of the earth, and the great men, and the rich men, and the chief captains, and the mighty men, and every bondman, and every free man, hid themselves in the dens and in the rocks of the mountains; 16 And said to the mountains and rocks, Fall on us, and hide us from the face of him that sitteth on the throne, and from the wrath of the Lamb: 17 For the great day of his wrath is come; and who shall be able to stand?"*

In Revelation 6:1-2 it says *"1 And I saw when the Lamb opened one of the seals, and I heard, as it were the noise of thunder, one of the four beasts saying, Come and see. 2 And I saw, and behold a white horse: and he that sat on him had a bow; and a crown was given unto him: and he went forth conquering, and to conquer."* In Revelation 6:1 the Lamb is Jesus Christ who is the only one worthy to open the seals. In Revelation 5:6-8 it says *"6 And I beheld, and, lo, in the midst of the throne and of the four beasts, and in the midst of the elders, stood a Lamb as it had been slain, having seven horns and seven eyes, which are the seven Spirits of God sent forth into all the earth. 7 And he came and took the book out of the right hand of him that sat upon the throne. 8 And when he had taken the book, the four beasts and four and twenty elders fell down before the Lamb, having every one of them harps, and golden vials full of odours, which are the prayers of saints."* Revelation 6:2 shows us when the first seal opened a white horse and on this horse is the Antichrist.

Some people mistakenly believe that Jesus is the one riding the horse in Revelation 6:2. This is not true. We must remember two things. First, that Jesus is opening these seven seals. Second, we must remember that Jesus Christ is coming to judge the world. Colossians 2:9-15 shows Jesus Christ's victory at the cross. In Colossians 2:9-15 it says *"9 For in him dwelleth all the fulness of the Godhead bodily. 10 And ye are complete in him, which is the head of all principality and power: 11 In whom also ye are circumcised with the circumcision made without hands, in putting off the body of the sins of the flesh by the circumcision of Christ: 12 Buried with him in baptism, wherein also ye are risen with him through the faith of the operation of God, who hath raised him from the dead. 13 And you, being dead in your sins and the uncircumcision of your flesh, hath he quickened together with him, having forgiven you all trespasses; 14 Blotting out the handwriting of ordinances that was against us, which was contrary to us, and took it out of the way, nailing it to his cross; 15 And having spoiled principalities and powers, he made a shew of them openly, triumphing over them in it."* Philippians 2:6-11 shows that after the death of Jesus Christ every knee shall bow and every tongue shall confess that He is Lord. In Philippians 2:6-11 it says *"6 Who, being in the form of God, thought it not robbery to be equal with God: 7 But made himself of no reputation, and took upon him the form of a servant, and was made in the likeness of men: 8 And being found in fashion as a man, he humbled himself, and became obedient unto death, even the death of the cross. 9 Wherefore God also hath highly exalted him, and given him a name which is above every name: 10 That at the name of Jesus every knee should bow, of things in heaven, and things in earth, and things under the earth; 11 And that every tongue should confess that Jesus Christ is Lord, to the glory of God the Father."* In Jude 14-15 it shows Jesus Christ coming with His saints to execute judgement on all. Jude 14-15 says *"14 And Enoch also, the seventh from Adam, prophesied of these, saying, Behold, the Lord cometh with ten thousands of his saints, 15 To execute judgment upon all, and to convince all that are ungodly among them of all their ungodly deeds which they have ungodly committed, and of all their hard speeches which ungodly sinners have spoken against him."* These scriptures show that there is no reason for Jesus to come and conquer. He has already conquered.

In Revelation 6:3-4 it says *"3 And when he had opened the second seal, I heard the second beast say, Come and see. 4 And there went out another horse that was red: and power was given to him that sat thereon to take peace from the earth, and that they should kill one another: and there was given unto him a great sword."* The red horse and the one that sits on this horse with a great sword is symbolic of war.

In Revelation 6:5-6 it says *"5 And when he had opened the third seal, I heard the third beast say, Come and see. And I beheld, and lo a black horse; and he that sat on him had a pair of balances in his hand. 6 And I heard a voice in the midst of the four beasts say, A measure of wheat for a penny, and three measures of barley for a penny; and see thou hurt not the oil and the wine."* The black horse and the one that sits on this horse with a pair of balances in his hand is symbolic of famine. A penny in the days of the apostle John equalled sixteen asses, so it is evident that a penny was worth a lot. Also a measure is equivalent to a peck and a half which equals 2 1/3 gallons. Revelation 6:6 shows very high food prices for a very small portion of food.

In Revelation 6:7-8 it says *"7 And when he had opened the fourth seal, I heard the voice of the fourth beast say, Come and see. 8 And I looked, and behold a pale horse: and his name that sat on him was Death, and Hell followed with him. And power was given unto them over the fourth part of the earth, to kill with sword, and with hunger, and with death, and with the beasts of the earth."* When the fourth seal is opened there comes a pale horse and his name that sat on him was Death and Hell. When this seal is opened death and destruction take over a fourth part of the earth.

In Revelation 6:9-11 it says " *9 And when he had opened the fifth seal, I saw under the altar the souls of them that were slain for the word of God, and for the testimony which they held: 10 And they cried with a loud voice, saying, How long, O Lord, holy and true, dost thou not judge and avenge our blood on them that dwell on the earth? 11 And white robes were given unto every one of them; and it was said unto them, that they should rest yet for a little season, until their fellowservants also and their brethren, that should be killed as they were, should be fulfilled.* " The opening of fifth seal shows Christians who will be killed for the cause of Jesus Christ. Jesus speaks how blessed are those who die in the Lord. In Revelation 14:13 it says *"And I heard a voice from heaven saying unto me, Write, Blessed are the dead which die in the Lord from henceforth: Yea, saith the Spirit, that they may rest from their labours; and their works do follow them."* In Revelation chapter 7 it confirms that the people in Revelation 6:10 are Christians in white robes killed for Christ. Revelation 7:9 says *"After this I beheld, and, lo, a great multitude, which no man could number, of all nations, and kindreds, and people, and tongues, stood before the throne, and before the Lamb, clothed with white robes, and palms in their hands;* Revelation 7:13-14 says: *13 And one of the elders answered, saying unto me, What are these which are arrayed in white robes? and whence came they? 14 And I said unto him, Sir, thou knowest. And he said to me, These are they which came out of great tribulation, and have washed their robes, and made them white in the blood of the Lamb."* Also Revelation chapter 3 shows the Christians in white. In Revelation 3:4-5 it says *"4 Thou hast a few names even in Sardis which have not defiled their garments; and they shall walk with me in white: for they are worthy. 5 He that overcometh, the same shall be clothed in white raiment; and I will not blot out his name out of the book of life, but I will confess his name before my Father, and before his angels."*

Page 73

In Revelation 6:12-17 it says *"12 And I beheld when he had opened the sixth seal, and, lo, there was a great earthquake; and the sun became black as sackcloth of hair, and the moon became as blood; 13 And the stars of heaven fell unto the earth, even as a fig tree casteth her untimely figs, when she is shaken of a mighty wind. 14 And the heaven departed as a scroll when it is rolled together; and every mountain and island were moved out of their places. 15 And the kings of the earth, and the great men, and the rich men, and the chief captains, and the mighty men, and every bondman, and every free man, hid themselves in the dens and in the rocks of the mountains; 16 And said to the mountains and rocks, Fall on us, and hide us from the face of him that sitteth on the throne, and from the wrath of the Lamb: 17 For the great day of his wrath is come; and who shall be able to stand?"* Verse 12 shows the sixth seal being opened and the sign that Jesus Christ showed us in Matthew 24:29-31.

(Refer to "The Signs In The Heavens Before Jesus Returns" on page 67 for more information). Also in Joel 3:15 it says *"15 The sun and the moon shall be darkened, and the stars shall withdraw their shining."* In Revelation 6:15-17 it shows how the kings of the earth and the great men hid themselves because God's wrath is about to come on the world. In Isaiah 2:19 shows us a similar picture of men hiding from the Lord. In Isaiah 2:19 it says *"And they shall go into the holes of the rocks, and into the caves of the earth, for fear of the LORD, and for the glory of his majesty, when he ariseth to shake terribly the earth."* Also in Zephaniah 1:14 it says *"The great day of the LORD is near, it is near, and hasteth greatly, even the voice of the day of the LORD: the mighty man shall cry there bitterly."*

The Sounding Of The Six Trumpets

In I Corinthians 15:15-52 the apostle Paul tells us that Jesus will return at the last trump or trumpet. In I Corinthians 15:51-52 it says *"Behold, I show you a mystery; We shall not all sleep, but we shall all be changed, in a moment, in the twinkling of an eye, at the last trump; for the trumpet shall sound, and the dead shall be raised incorruptible, and we shall be changed."* This means all six trumpets will sound before the return of Jesus Christ. In Revelation chapter 8 and 9 it shows trumpets one through six sound. In Revelation 8:6-13 it says *"6 And the seven angels which had the seven trumpets prepared themselves to sound. 7 The first angel sounded, and there followed hail and fire mingled with blood, and they were cast upon the earth: and the third part of trees was burnt up, and all green grass was burnt up. 8 And the second angel sounded, and as it were a great mountain burning with fire was cast into the sea: and the third part of the sea became blood; 9 And the third part of the creatures which were in the sea, and had life, died; and the third part of the ships were destroyed. 10 And the third angel sounded, and there fell a great star from heaven, burning as it were a lamp, and it fell upon the third part of the rivers, and upon the fountains of waters; 11 And the name of the star is called Wormwood: and the third part of the waters became wormwood; and many men died of the waters, because they were made bitter. 12 And the fourth angel sounded, and the third part of the sun was smitten, and the third part of the moon, and the third part of the stars; so as the third part of them was darkened, and the day shone not for a third part of it, and the night likewise. 13 And I beheld, and heard an angel flying through the midst of heaven, saying with a loud voice, Woe, woe, woe, to the inhabiters of the earth by reason of the other voices of the trumpet of the three angels, which are yet to sound!"*

In Revelation 8:7 it says *"7 The first angel sounded, and there followed hail and fire mingled with blood, and they were cast upon the earth: and the third part of trees was burnt up, and all green grass was burnt up."* The first trumpet sounded and notice there is no mention of the church leaving (Refer to "The Pre-Rapture Or First Trumpet Message" on page 13 for more information).

In Revelation 8:8-9 it says *"8 And the second angel sounded, and as it were a great mountain burning with fire was cast into the sea: and the third part of the sea became blood; 9 And the third part of the creatures which were in the sea, and had life, died; and the third part of the ships were destroyed."* The second trumpet sounded and look at God's judgement on the earth and the things that are in the earth.

In Revelation 8:10-11 it says *"10 And the third angel sounded, and there fell a great star from heaven, burning as it were a lamp, and it fell upon the third part of the rivers, and upon the fountains of waters; 11 And the name of the star is called Wormwood: and the third part of the waters became wormwood; and many men died of the waters, because they were made bitter."* The third trumpet sounded we see more judgement and many men dying of the waters.

In Revelation 8:12 it says *"And the fourth angel sounded, and the third part of the sun was smitten, and the third part of the moon, and the third part of the stars; so as the third part of them was darkened, and the day shone not for a third part of it, and the night likewise."* Verse 12 shows the fourth trumpet sound and the sign that Jesus Christ showed us in Matthew 24:29-31.

(Refer to "The Signs In The Heavens Before Jesus Returns" in this chapter for more information). Also in Isaiah 13:10 it says

"For the stars of heaven and the constellations thereof shall not give their light: the sun shall be darkened in his going forth, and the moon shall not cause her light to shine." In chapter 9 of the book of Revelation it shows us the fifth and sixth trumpet sounding. In Revelation 9:1-21 it says *"1 And the fifth angel sounded, and I saw a star fall from heaven unto the earth: and to him was given the key of the bottomless pit. 2 And he opened the bottomless pit; and there arose a smoke out of the pit, as the smoke of a great furnace; and the sun and the air were darkened by reason of the smoke of the pit. 3 And there came out of the smoke locusts upon the earth: and unto them was given power, as the scorpions of the earth have power. 4 And it was commanded them that they should not hurt the grass of the earth, neither any green thing, neither any tree; but only those men which have not the seal of God in their foreheads. 5 And to them it was given that they should not kill them, but that they should be tormented five months: and their torment was as the torment of a scorpion, when he striketh a man. 6 And in those days shall men seek death, and shall not find it; and shall desire to die, and death shall flee from them. 7 And the shapes of the locusts were like unto horses prepared unto battle; and on their heads were as it were crowns like gold, and their faces were as the faces of men. 8 And they had hair as the hair of women, and their teeth were as the teeth of lions. 9 And they had breastplates, as it were breastplates of iron; and the sound of their wings was as the sound of chariots of many horses running to battle. 10 And they had tails like unto scorpions, and there were stings in their tails: and their power was to hurt men five months. 11 And they had a king over them, which is the angel of the bottomless pit, whose name in the Hebrew tongue is Abaddon, but in the Greek tongue hath his name Apollyon. 12 One woe is past; and, behold, there come two woes more hereafter. 13 And the sixth angel sounded, and I heard a voice from the four horns of the golden altar which is before God, 14 Saying to the sixth angel which had the trumpet, Loose the four*

angels which are bound in the great river Euphrates. 15 And the four angels were loosed, which were prepared for an hour, and a day, and a month, and a year, for to slay the third part of men. 16 And the number of the army of the horsemen were two hundred thousand thousand: and I heard the number of them. 17 And thus I saw the horses in the vision, and them that sat on them, having breastplates of fire, and of jacinth, and brimstone: and the heads of the horses were as the heads of lions; and out of their mouths issued fire and smoke and brimstone. 18 By these three was the third part of men killed, by the fire, and by the smoke, and by the brimstone, which issued out of their mouths. 19 For their power is in their mouth, and in their tails: for their tails were like unto serpents, and had heads, and with them they do hurt. 20 And the rest of the men which were not killed by these plagues yet repented not of the works of their hands, that they should not worship devils, and idols of gold, and silver, and brass, and stone, and of wood: which neither can see, nor hear, nor walk: 21 Neither repented they of their murders, nor of their sorceries, nor of their fornication, nor of their thefts. "

In Revelation 9:1-10 the fifth trumpet sounded and locusts were to hurt the men which have not the seal of God in their foreheads for five months upon the earth. In Revelation 9:4 it says *"4 And it was commanded them that they should not hurt the grass of the earth, neither any green thing, neither any tree; but only those men which have not the seal of God in their foreheads. "* Just as God protected his people the children of Israel in the old testament God will protect the true Christians in this time of judgement.

In Revelation 9:13-21 the sixth trumpet sounded and a third of men were killed on the earth. In Revelation 9:15 it says *"15 And the four angels were loosed, which were prepared for an hour, and a day, and a month, and a year, for to slay the third part of men.*" After all these plagues we see that men still will not repent. In Revelation 9:20-21 it says *"20 And the rest of the men which were not killed by these plagues yet repented not of the works of their hands, that they should not worship devils, and idols of gold, and silver, and brass, and stone, and of wood: which neither can see, nor hear, nor walk: 21 Neither repented they of their murders, nor of their sorceries, nor of their fornication, nor of their thefts."*

The Two Witnesses

Who Are The Two Witnesses?

The two witnesses are Elijah and Moses which will be on the earth for almost 3 -1/2 years. In Revelation 11:3-6 it says *"3 And I will give power unto my two witnesses, and they shall prophesy a thousand two hundred and threescore days, clothed in sackcloth. 4 These are the two olive trees, and the two candlesticks standing before the God of the earth. 5 And if any man will hurt them, fire proceedeth out of their mouth, and devoureth their enemies: and if any man will hurt them, he must in this manner be killed. 6 These have power to shut heaven, that it rain not in the days of their prophecy: and have power over waters to turn them to blood, and to smite the earth with all plagues, as often as they will."* From verse 3 we see that the two witnesses shall prophesy a thousand two hundred threescore days or 3 years 165 days.

We can confirm who these two witnesses are by looking in the gospel of Matthew. When Jesus Christ was transfigured, Elijah and Moses were there with Him. In Matthew 17:1-8 it says *"1 And after six days Jesus taketh Peter, James, and John his brother, and bringeth them up into an high mountain apart, 2 And was transfigured before them: and his face did shine as the sun, and his raiment was white as the light. 3 And, behold, there appeared unto them Moses and Elias talking with him. 4 Then answered Peter, and said unto Jesus, Lord, it is good for us to be here: if thou wilt, let us make here three tabernacles; one for thee, and one for Moses, and one for Elias. 5 While he yet spake, behold, a bright cloud overshadowed them: and behold a voice out of the cloud, which said, This is my beloved Son, in whom I am well pleased; hear ye him. 6 And when the disciples heard it, they fell on their face, and were sore afraid. 7 And Jesus came and touched them, and said, Arise, and be not afraid. 8 And when they had lifted up their eyes, they saw no man, save Jesus only."*

We can also confirm who the two witnesses are by looking at what Elijah and Moses did when they were living on the earth and compare this to what the two witnesses will do in the future. Revelation speaks about the two witnesses calling fire down from heaven. Revelation 11:4-5 says *"4 These are the two olive trees, and the two candlesticks standing before the God of the earth. 5 And if any man will hurt them, fire proceedeth out of their mouth, and devoureth their enemies: and if any man will hurt them, he must in this manner be killed."*

Compare this to Elijah. Elijah was used to call fire down from heaven. In I Kings 18:37-40 it says *"37 Hear me, O LORD, hear me, that this people may know that thou art the LORD God, and that thou hast turned their heart back again. 38 Then the fire of the LORD fell, and consumed the burnt sacrifice, and the wood, and the stones, and the dust, and licked up the water that was in the trench. 39 And when all the people saw it, they fell on their faces: and they said, The LORD, he is the God; the LORD, he is the God. 40 And Elijah said unto them, Take the prophets of Baal; let not one of them escape. And they took them: and Elijah brought them down to the brook Kishon, and slew them there."*

Elijah also called fire down from heaven on another occasion. In II Kings 1:9-12 it says *"9 Then the king sent unto him a captain of fifty with his fifty. And he went up to him: and, behold, he sat on the top of an hill. And he spake unto him, Thou man of God, the king hath said, Come down. 10 And Elijah answered and said to the captain of fifty, If I be a man of God, then let fire come down from heaven, and consume thee and thy fifty. And there came down fire from heaven, and consumed him and his fifty. 11 Again also he sent unto him another captain of fifty with his fifty. And he answered and said unto him, O man of God, thus hath the king said, Come down quickly. 12 And Elijah answered and said unto them, If I be a man of God, let fire come down from heaven, and consume thee and thy fifty. And the fire of God came down from heaven, and consumed him and his fifty."*

Revelation also speaks about the two witnesses shutting the heavens so that no rain falls, and also about the two witnesses turning water into blood. In Revelation 11:6 it says *"These have power to shut heaven, that it rain not in the days of their prophecy: and have power over waters to turn them to blood, and to smite the earth with all plagues, as often as they will."*

We can compare this verse in Revelation to what God did through Elijah and Moses in the Old Testament. The prophet Elijah spoke about a famine in the days of king Ahab. This famine lasted 3 -1/2 years. In I Kings 17:1 it says *" And Elijah the Tishbite, who was of the inhabitants of Gilead, said unto Ahab, As the LORD God of Israel liveth, before whom I stand, there shall not be dew nor rain these years, but according to my word."* In James 5:17-18 it shows the time frame of 3-1/2 years of this famine. In James 5:17-18 it says *"17 Elias was a man subject to like passions as we are, and he prayed earnestly that it might not rain: and it rained not on the earth by the space of three years and six months. 18 And he prayed again, and the heaven gave rain, and the earth brought forth her fruit.* "The prophet Moses was used to send the plagues in Egypt. The first plague Moses turned the water into blood. In Exodus 7:19-24 it says *"19 And the LORD spake unto Moses, Say unto Aaron, Take thy rod, and stretch out thine hand upon the waters of Egypt, upon their streams, upon their rivers, and upon their ponds, and upon all their pools of water, that they may become blood; and that there may be blood throughout all the land of Egypt, both in vessels of wood, and in vessels of stone. 20 And Moses and Aaron did so, as the LORD commanded; and he lifted up the rod, and smote the waters that were in the river, in the sight of Pharaoh, and in the sight of his servants; and all the waters that were in the river were turned to blood. 21 And the fish that was in the river died; and the river stank, and the Egyptians could not drink of the water of the river; and there was blood throughout all the land of Egypt. 22 And the magicians of Egypt did so with their enchantments: and Pharaoh's heart was hardened, neither did he hearken unto them; as the LORD had said. 23 And Pharaoh turned and went into his house, neither did he set his heart to this also. 24 And all the Egyptians digged round about the river for water to drink; for they could not drink of the water of the river."*

It is evident by comparing these scriptures that Elijah and Moses are the two witnesses.

How Do We Know That The Two Witnesses Will Be On The Earth Before The Return Of Jesus Christ?

After the two witnesses are killed by the Antichrist and they ascend into heaven, the Bible shows us that the second woe is past. In Revelation 11:7-14 it says *"7 And when they shall have finished their testimony, the beast that ascendeth out of the bottomless pit shall make war against them, and shall overcome them, and kill them. 8 And their dead bodies shall lie in the street of the great city, which spiritually is called Sodom and Egypt, where also our Lord was crucified. 9 And they of the people and kindreds and tongues and nations shall see their dead bodies three days and an half, and shall not suffer their dead bodies to be put in graves. 10 And they that dwell upon the earth shall rejoice over them, and make merry, and shall send gifts one to another; because these two prophets tormented them that dwelt on the earth. 11 And after three days and an half the Spirit of life from God entered into them, and they stood upon their feet; and great fear fell upon them which saw them. 12 And they heard a great voice from heaven saying unto them, Come up hither. And they ascended up to heaven in a cloud; and their enemies beheld them. 13 And the same hour was there a great earthquake, and the tenth part of the city fell, and in the earthquake were slain of men seven thousand: and the remnant were affrighted, and gave glory to the God of heaven. 14 The second woe is past; and, behold, the third woe cometh quickly."*

This is key in understanding the timing of the two witnesses. In Revelation 8:13 the Bible mentions three woes. Revelation 8:13 says *"And I beheld, and heard an angel flying through the midst of heaven, saying with a loud voice, Woe, woe, woe, to the inhabiters of the earth by reason of the other voices of the trumpet of the three angels, which are yet to sound!"* Each woe is past after the fifth, sixth and seventh trumpets sound. So when the fifth trumpet sounds, one woe is past. When the sixth trumpet sounds the second woe is past and when the seventh trumpet sounds the third woe is past. In Revelation 9:12 the fifth trumpet has sounded and one woe has passed. Revelation 9:12 says *"One woe is past; and, behold, there come two woes more hereafter."* In Revelation 11:14 the third woe or seventh trumpet has not sounded which shows us that at the same time the trumpets are sounding the two witnesses are on the earth which is before the return of Jesus Christ. In Revelation 11:14 it says *"The second woe is past; and, behold, the third woe cometh quickly."*

The Rise To Power Of The Great Whore

Revelation chapter 17 shows us Satan's Church, the great whore. This is the religious system Satan will use in the last days. In Revelation 17:1-6 it says *"1 And there came one of the seven angels which had the seven vials, and talked with me, saying unto me, Come hither; I will shew unto thee the judgment of the great whore that sitteth upon many waters: 2 With whom the kings of the earth have committed fornication, and the inhabitants of the earth have been made drunk with the wine of her fornication. 3 So he carried me away in the spirit into the wilderness: and I saw a woman sit upon a scarlet coloured beast, full of names of blasphemy, having seven heads and ten horns. 4 And the woman was arrayed in purple and scarlet colour, and decked with gold and precious stones and pearls, having a golden cup in her hand full of abominations and filthiness of her fornication: 5 And upon her forehead was a name written, MYSTERY, BABYLON THE GREAT, THE MOTHER OF HARLOTS AND ABOMINATIONS OF THE EARTH. 6 And I saw the woman drunken with the blood of the saints, and with the blood of the martyrs of Jesus: and when I saw her, I wondered with great admiration."*

Revelation 17:1 shows the great whore sitting upon many waters. These waters are peoples, multitudes, nations and tongues. In Revelation 17:15 it says *"And he saith unto me, The waters which thou sawest, where the whore sitteth, are peoples, and multitudes, and nations, and tongues."*

Revelation 17:2-3 describes the great whore. This passage says *"2 With whom the kings of the earth have committed fornication, and the inhabitants of the earth have been made drunk with the wine of her fornication. 3 So he carried me away in the spirit into the wilderness: and I saw a woman sit upon a scarlet coloured beast, full of names of blasphemy, having seven heads and ten horns."* Revelation 17:9 explains who this great whore or woman is that is riding on the beast (The beast is the Antichrist). Revelation 17:9 says *"And here is the mind which hath wisdom. The seven heads are seven mountains, on which the woman sitteth."* The only place in the world that is described as having seven mountains is Rome in Italy. Revelation 17:18 says *"And the woman which thou sawest is that great city, which reigneth over the kings of the earth."* This woman is the Roman Catholic church which is headed by the Pope. The Pope not only heads the Roman Catholic church, but he also has great influence over the false religions of the world.

In Revelation 17:4-5 it says *"4 And the woman was arrayed in purple and scarlet colour, and decked with gold and precious stones and pearls, having a golden cup in her hand full of abominations and filthiness of her fornication: 5 And upon her forehead was a name written, MYSTERY, BABYLON THE GREAT, THE MOTHER OF HARLOTS AND ABOMINATIONS OF THE EARTH."* We are seeing *" MYSTERY, BABYLON THE GREAT, THE MOTHER OF HARLOTS AND ABOMINATIONS OF THE EARTH"* being formed right before our very eyes under the ecumenical movement. A recent article in June 6, 1999 edition of The Oregonian Newspaper was titled "John Paul II returns to stable Poland". This article states "Ninety-five percent of Poles are Catholic, and 75 percent describe themselves as practicing followers, making Poland one of the most devout countries in Europe. The Pope, who is to meet on several occasions with religious leaders of different faiths -- Eastern Orthodox, Jewish, Lutheran and Muslim -- will preach an ecumenical message to a country that has not had much practical experience in reaching out." Note that the Pope is not only reaching out to Catholics, but to people from all different religions as well. This is not building the church of Jesus Christ but it is the great whore of false religions unifying with Satan to form a one world religion.

Many Christian leaders are adopting the ecumenical viewpoint and are preaching unity at any cost. They say that it is not what you believe in that matters but that we must be in unity. Jesus Christ spoke concerning the religious leaders in His day. In Matthew 16:6-12 it says *"6 Then Jesus said unto them, Take heed and beware of the leaven of the Pharisees and of the Sadducees. 7 And they reasoned among themselves, saying, It is because we have taken no bread. 8 Which when Jesus perceived, he said unto them, O ye of little faith, why reason ye among yourselves, because ye have brought no bread? 9 Do ye not yet understand, neither remember the five loaves of the five thousand, and how many baskets ye took up? 10 Neither the seven loaves of the four thousand, and how many baskets ye took up? 11 How is it that ye do not understand that I spake it not to you concerning bread, that ye should beware of the leaven of the Pharisees and of the Sadducees? 12 Then understood they how that he bade them not beware of the leaven of bread, but of the doctrine of the Pharisees and of the Sadducees."* The apostle Paul also told us in Galatians 1:6-8 *"I marvel that ye are so soon removed from him that called you into the grace of Christ unto another gospel: Which is not another; but there be some that trouble you, and would pervert the gospel of Christ. But though we, or an angel from heaven, preach any other gospel unto you than that which we have preached unto you, let him be accursed."* In I Corinthians 1:10 the apostle Paul tells us we must first speak the same thing. In I Corinthians 1:10 it says *"Now I beseech you, brethren, by the name of our Lord Jesus Christ, that ye all speak the same thing,* and that there be no divisions among you; but that ye be perfectly joined together in the same mind and in the same judgment." Jesus Christ and the apostles warned us concerning false doctrine. Don't be deceived by Christian leaders who are preaching unity regardless of beliefs. You will be tricked into becoming a part of Satan's church.

The Rise To Power Of The Revived Roman Empire

In both the book of Revelation and the book of Daniel , God reveals that the final, worldly kingdom will be the Revived Roman Empire. In Daniel 7:1-7, Daniel spoke of four kingdoms that would come upon the earth. These four kingdoms are: Babylon, Media-Persia, Greece and Rome. Daniel 7:7 and 7:23-24 show us that the fourth kingdom (or fourth beast) in the Bible is the original Roman empire. Daniel 7:7 states *"After this I saw in the night visions, and behold a fourth beast, dreadful and terrible, and strong exceedingly; and it had great iron teeth: it devoured and brake in pieces, and stamped the residue with the feet of it: and it was diverse from all the beasts that were before it; and it had ten horns."* Daniel 7:23-24 says *"Thus he said, the fourth beast shall be the fourth kingdom upon earth, which shall be diverse from all kingdoms, and shall devour the whole earth, and shall tread it down, and break it in pieces. And the ten horns out of this kingdom are ten kings that shall arise: and another shall rise after them; and he shall be diverse from the first, and he shall subdue three kings."*

On Jan. 1,1999, eleven European nations united their economies. These nations are Austria, Belgium, Finland, France, Germany, Ireland, Italy, Luxembourg, the Netherlands, Spain and Portugal with four nations possibly joining by Jan. 1, 2002. These four nations are Britain, Denmark, Sweden and Greece. These 15 nations are becoming one nation economically. The land that these 15 nations occupy is almost identical to the land occupied by the original Roman Empire from 44 B.C. to 117 A.D. These nations are called the European Union. Revelation 17:12-13 shows us the final kingdom, European Union which is the also known as the Revived Roman Empire. Revelation 17:12-13 says *"And the ten horns which thou sawest are ten kings, which have received no kingdom as yet; but receive power as kings one hour with the beast. These have one mind, and shall give their power and strength unto the beast."* This scripture also confirms that the final kingdom is the European Union, because the European Union has not come into its full power yet. It is waiting for the Antichrist.

The Falling Away Of The Church

In II Thessalonians 2:3 the apostle Paul tells us that there would be a falling away of the church before the return of Jesus Christ. II Thessalonians 2:3 says *"Let no man deceive you by any means: for that day shall not come, expect there come a falling away first, and that man of sin be revealed, the son of perdition;"* Paul also spoke about this in I Timothy 4:1 which says *"Now the Spirit speaketh expressly, that in the latter times some shall depart from the faith, giving heed to seducing spirits, and doctrines of devils."* For more information on this topic see "The Pensacola/Toronto Revival Or Falling Away" on page 15.

The Man Of Sin Being Revealed (Antichrist)

In II Thessalonians 2:3 the apostle Paul tells us that before the return of Jesus Christ the man of sin would be revealed. In II Thessalonians 2:3 it says *"Let no man deceive you by any means: for that day shall not come, expect there come a falling away first, and that man of sin be revealed, the son of perdition;"* This man of sin is the Antichrist. The Webster's Dictionary defines the word reveal as "to make known what was hidden or secret."

Many may wonder when will the world know who the Antichrist really is? We will know who he is because the Antichrist has a false resurrection which is described in Revelation 13:3. This verse says *"And I saw one of his heads as it were wounded to death; and his deadly wound was healed: and all the world wondered after the beast."* Also in Revelation 13:14 it says *"And deceiveth them that dwell on the earth by the means of those miracles which he had power to do in the sight of the beast; saying to them that dwell on the earth, that they should make an image to the beast, which had the wound by a sword, and did live."* This will happen at the end of the first 3-1/2 years of the tribulation. In the section of this chapter titled "The Two Witnesses" it is the Antichrist who kills the two witnesses after they have finished their testimony. In Revelation 11:7 it says *" And when they shall have finished their testimony, the beast that ascendeth out of the bottomless pit shall make war against them, and shall overcome them, and kill them."* The two witnesses are on the earth for almost 3- 1/2 years or 1260 days (which is 3 years 165 days) (refer to "How Do We Know That The Two Witnesses Will Be On The Earth Before The Return Of Jesus Christ" on page 82 for more information).

The Return Of Jesus Christ

The Seventh Trumpet

In I Thessalonians 4:13-18 Paul shows us the church being caught away to meet the Lord in the air. In I Thessalonians 4:13-18 it says *"13 But I would not have you to be ignorant, brethren, concerning them which are asleep, that ye sorrow not, even as others which have no hope. 14 For if we believe that Jesus died and rose again, even so them also which sleep in Jesus will God bring with him. 15 For this we say unto you by the word of the Lord, that we which are alive and remain unto the coming of the Lord shall not prevent them which are asleep. 16 For the Lord himself shall descend from heaven with a shout, with the voice of the archangel, and with the trump of God: and the dead in Christ shall rise first: 17 Then we which are alive and remain shall be caught up together with them in the clouds, to meet the Lord in the air: and so shall we ever be with the Lord. 18 Wherefore comfort one another with these words."* In I Corinthians 15:51-52 the apostle Paul tells us that this will be at the last trump or trumpet.   In I Corinthians 15:51-52 it says *"Behold, I show you a mystery; We shall not all sleep, but we shall all be changed, in a moment, in the twinkling of an eye, at the last trump; for the trumpet shall sound, and the dead shall be raised incorruptible, and we shall be changed."* In the book of Revelation it mentions seven trumpets and when the seventh trumpet sounds the church will be caught away to be with Jesus Christ. In Revelation 10 :7 it says *" But in the days of the voice of the seventh angel, when he shall begin to sound, the mystery of God should be finished, as he hath declared to his servants the prophets."* Notice when the seventh trumpet begins to sounds the mystery of God should be finished. Revelation 11:15-18 shows us the time after the seven trumpets have sounded and the church is with Jesus Christ receiving their rewards.   This is the time of the Judgement seat of Christ and of God's wrath coming on the world. In Revelation 11:15-18 it says *"15 And the seventh angel sounded; and there were great voices in heaven, saying, The kingdoms of this world are become the kingdoms of our Lord, and of his Christ; and he shall reign for ever and ever. 16 And the four and twenty elders, which sat before God on their seats, fell upon their faces, and worshipped God, 17 Saying, We give thee thanks, O Lord God Almighty, which art, and wast, and art to come; because thou hast taken to thee thy great power, and hast reigned. 18 And the nations were angry, and thy wrath is come, and the time of the dead, that they should be judged, and that thou shouldest give reward unto thy servants the prophets, and to the saints, and them that fear thy name, small and great; and shouldest destroy them which destroy the earth."*

The Seventh Seal

When the seventh seal is opened it shows us another confirmation of the Christians receiving their rewards or the Judgement seat of Christ. In Revelation 8:1 it says *"And when he had opened the seventh seal, there was silence in heaven about the space of half an hour."* The only time there will be silence in heaven will be for the Judgement seat of Christ. If you refer back to the section of this chapter titled "The Opening Of The Six Seals" (page 68) you will see that God's wrath is about to be poured on the earth. When the seventh trumpet sounds, as discussed on the previous topic, it shows the Christians receiving their rewards and the wrath of God coming on the earth. The apostle Paul spoke about the Judgement seat of Christ in II Corinthians 5:10 and in Romans 14:10. In II Corinthians 5:10 it says *"For we must all appear before the judgment seat of Christ; that every one may receive the things done in his body, according to that he hath done, whether it be good or bad."* Also in Romans 14:10 it says *"But why dost thou judge thy brother? or why dost thou set at nought thy brother? for we shall all stand before the judgment seat of Christ."* In I Corinthians 3:11-15 the apostle Paul shows the rewards and the works that will be burned. In I Corinthians 3:11-15 it says *"11 For other foundation can no man lay than that is laid, which is Jesus Christ. 12 Now if any man build upon this foundation gold, silver, precious stones, wood, hay, stubble; 13 Every man's work shall be made manifest: for the day shall declare it, because it shall be revealed by fire; and the fire shall try every man's work of what sort it is. 14 If any man's work abide which he hath built thereupon, he shall receive a reward. 15 If any man's work shall be burned, he shall suffer loss: but he himself shall be saved; yet so as by fire."* Notice in verses 14 and 15 how even though his works were burned he did not lose his soul.

CHAPTER 6

Satan Is A Counterfeit Of God

For such are false apostles, deceitful workers, transforming themselves into the apostles of Christ. And no marvel; for Satan himself is transformed into an angel of light. Therefore it is no great thing if his ministers also be transformed as the ministers of righteousness; whose end shall be according to their works
II Corinthians 11:13-15

In this chapter we will show you how Satan is a counterfeit of God. In each of the nine sub-topics below, part a will show a characteristic of God and part b will show what Satan's counterfeit is.

Age

a)Jesus Was 30 When His Ministry Began - In Luke 3:23 it says *"And Jesus himself began to be about thirty years of age, being (as was supposed) the son of Joseph, which was the son of Heli,"* (refer to Chapter. 9 under "Sixty-Nine Weeks Of The Seventy Weeks Have Been Fulfilled" for another confirmation)

b) Antichrist Is 30 When He Comes Into Power - The Lord Jesus Christ spoke to me through a word of wisdom that the Antichrist will be 30 years old.

3-1/2 years

a) Jesus' Earthly Ministry Was 3 -1/2 Years - In Daniel 9:27 it says *"And he shall confirm the covenant with many for one week: and in the midst of the week he shall cause the sacrifice and the oblation to cease, and for the overspreading of abominations he shall make it desolate, even until the consummation, and that determined shall be poured upon the desolate."* I will go into more detail in Chapter 9 under the topic titled "Seventy Weeks."

b) Antichrist - The Antichrist will have a false peace for the first 3-1/2 years. In Daniel 8:23-26 it says *"23 And in the latter time of their kingdom, when the transgressors are come to the full, a king of fierce countenance, and understanding dark sentences, shall stand up. 24 And his power shall be mighty, but not by his own power: and he shall destroy wonderfully, and shall prosper, and practise, and shall destroy the mighty and the holy people. 25 And through his policy also he shall cause craft to prosper in his hand; and he shall magnify himself in his heart, and by peace shall destroy many: he shall also stand up against the Prince of princes; but he shall be broken without hand. 26 And the vision of the evening and the morning which was told is true: wherefore shut thou up the vision; for it shall be for many days."* (refer to Chapter 5 under "The Man Of Sin Being Revealed" on page 88 for another confirmation of the first 3-1/2 years of time).

In The Flesh

a) Jesus Was God In The Flesh - John 1:1 and 1:14 say *"1 In the beginning was the Word, and the Word was with God, and the Word was God. 14 And the Word was made flesh, and dwelt among us, (and we beheld his glory, the glory as of the only begotten of the Father,) full of grace and truth."*

b) Antichrist - The Antichrist will be Satan in the flesh. - Revelation 13:2 says *"And the beast which I saw was like unto a leopard, and his feet were as the feet of a bear, and his mouth as the mouth of a lion: and the dragon gave him his power, and his seat, and great authority."* The dragon is the Devil as explained in Revelation 12:9.

Resurrection

a) Jesus Was Resurrected - Matthew 28:1-6 says *"1 In the end of the sabbath, as it began to dawn toward the first day of the week, came Mary Magdalene and the other Mary to see the sepulchre. 2 And, behold, there was a great earthquake: for the angel of the Lord descended from heaven, and came and rolled back the stone from the door, and sat upon it. 3 His countenance was like lightning, and his raiment white as snow: 4 And for fear of him the keepers did shake, and became as dead men. 5 And the angel answered and said unto the women, Fear not ye: for I know that ye seek Jesus, which was crucified. 6 He is not here: for he is risen, as he said. Come, see the place where the Lord lay.*

b) Antichrist - The Antichrist will have a false resurrection.- Revelation 13:3 says *"And I saw one of his heads as it were wounded to death; and his deadly wound was healed: and all the world wondered after the beast."*

We Have The Holy Ghost

a) Holy Ghost - John 16:13-14 says *"13 Howbeit when he, the Spirit of truth, is come, he will guide you into all truth: for he shall not speak of himself; but whatsoever he shall hear, that shall he speak: and he will shew you things to come. 14 He shall glorify me: for he shall receive of mine, and shall shew it unto you."* The Holy Ghost will only lift up Jesus.

b) False Prophet - Revelation 13:11-12 says *"11 And I beheld another beast coming up out of the earth; and he had two horns like a lamb, and he spake as a dragon. 12 And he exerciseth all the power of the first beast before him, and causeth the earth and them which dwell therein to worship the first beast, whose deadly wound was healed.*

Revelation 19:20 says *And the beast was taken, and with him the false prophet that wrought miracles before him, with which he deceived them that had received the mark of the beast, and them that worshipped his image. These both were cast alive into a lake of fire burning with brimstone."* Satan has the false prophet who will lift up the Antichrist.

A Covenant With Israel

a) God Signed A Covenant With Israel - Exodus 6:2-5 says *"2 And God spake unto Moses, and said unto him, I am the LORD: 3 And I appeared unto Abraham, unto Isaac, and unto Jacob, by the name of God Almighty, but by my name JEHOVAH was I not known to them. 4 And I have also established my covenant with them, to give them the land of Canaan, the land of their pilgrimage, wherein they were strangers. 5 And I have also heard the groaning of the children* of Israel, whom the Egyptians keep in bondage; and I have remembered my covenant."

b) Antichrist - The Antichrist will make a covenant with Israel. Daniel 11:32 says *"And such as do wickedly against the covenant shall he corrupt by flatteries: but the people that do know their God shall be strong, and do exploits."* Jesus Christ spoke in John 5:43 about the Jewish people receiving the Antichrist. In John 5:43 it says *"I am come in my Father's name, and ye receive me not: if another shall come in his own name, him ye will receive."*

A True Kingdom And A False Kingdom

a) God Is Going To Set Up His Kingdom - Revelation 21:1-7 says *"1 And I saw a new heaven and a new earth: for the first heaven and the first earth were passed away; and there was no more sea. 2 And I John saw the holy city, new Jerusalem, coming down from God out of heaven, prepared as a bride adorned for her husband. 3 And I heard a great voice out of heaven saying, Behold, the tabernacle of God is with men, and he will dwell with them, and they shall be his people, and God himself shall be with them, and be their God. 4 And God shall wipe away all tears from their eyes; and there shall be no more death, neither sorrow, nor crying, neither shall there be any more pain: for the former things are passed away. 5 And he that sat upon the throne said, Behold, I make all things new. And he said unto me, Write: for these words are true and faithful. 6 And he said unto me, It is done. I am Alpha and Omega, the beginning and the end. I will give unto him that is athirst of the fountain of the water of life freely. 7 He that overcometh shall inherit all things; and I will be his God, and he shall be my son.*

Revelation 21:22-27 says *22 And I saw no temple therein: for the Lord God Almighty and the Lamb are the temple of it. 23*

And the city had no need of the sun, neither of the moon, to shine in it: for the glory of God did lighten it, and the Lamb is the light thereof. 24 And the nations of them which are saved shall walk in the light of it: and the kings of the earth do bring their glory and honour into it. 25 And the gates of it shall not be shut at all by day: for there shall be no night there. 26 And they shall bring the glory and honour of the nations into it. 27 And there shall in no wise enter into it any thing that defileth, neither whatsoever worketh abomination, or maketh a lie: but they which are written in the Lamb's book of life."

In Zechariah 14:16 it says *"And it shall come to pass, that every one that is left of all the nations which came against Jerusalem shall even go up from year to year to worship the King, the LORD of hosts, and to keep the feast of tabernacles."*

b) Satan Tries To Set Up His Kingdom - Revelation 17:1-18 says *"1 And there came one of the seven angels which had the seven vials, and talked with me, saying unto me, Come hither; I will shew unto thee the judgment of the great whore that sitteth upon many waters: 2 With whom the kings of the earth have committed fornication, and the inhabitants of the earth have been made drunk with the wine of her fornication. 3 So he carried me away in the spirit into the wilderness: and I saw a woman sit upon a scarlet coloured beast, full of names of blasphemy, having seven heads and ten horns. 4 And the woman was arrayed in purple and scarlet colour, and decked with gold and precious stones and pearls, having a golden cup in her hand full of abominations and filthiness of her fornication: 5 And upon her forehead was a name written, MYSTERY, BABYLON THE GREAT, THE MOTHER OF HARLOTS AND ABOMINATIONS OF THE EARTH. 6 And I saw the woman drunken with the blood of the saints, and with the blood of the martyrs of Jesus: and when I saw her, I wondered with great admiration. 7 And the angel said unto me,*

Wherefore didst thou marvel? I will tell thee the mystery of the woman, and of the beast that carrieth her, which hath the seven heads and ten horns. 8 The beast that thou sawest was, and is not; and shall ascend out of the bottomless pit, and go into perdition: and they that dwell on the earth shall wonder, whose names were not written in the book of life from the foundation of the world, when they behold the beast that was, and is not, and yet is. 9 And here is the mind which hath wisdom. The seven heads are seven mountains, on which the woman sitteth. 10 And there are seven kings: five are fallen, and one is, and the other is not yet come; and when he cometh, he must continue a short space. 11 And the beast that was, and is not, even he is the eighth, and is of the seven, and goeth into perdition. 12 And the ten horns which thou sawest are ten kings, which have received no kingdom as yet; but receive power as kings one hour with the beast. 13 These have one mind, and shall give their power and strength unto the beast. 14 These shall make war with the Lamb, and the Lamb shall overcome them: for he is Lord of lords, and King of kings: and they that are with him are called, and chosen, and faithful. 15 And he saith unto me, The waters which thou sawest, where the whore sitteth, are peoples, and multitudes, and nations, and tongues. 16 And the ten horns which thou sawest upon the beast, these shall hate the whore, and shall make her desolate and naked, and shall eat her flesh, and burn her with fire. 17 For God hath put in their hearts to fulfil his will, and to agree, and give their kingdom unto the beast, until the words of God shall be fulfilled. 18 And the woman which thou sawest is that great city, which reigneth over the kings of the earth."

This passage of scripture shows how Satan tries to set up his kingdom through the Antichrist (Revelation 17:13 and 17), the whore or Satan's church (Revelation 17:9) and the Revived Roman Empire (Revelation 17:12). Chapter 5 titled "What Prophecies Must Be Fulfilled Before Jesus Christ's Return," provides more detail on the prophecies which need to be fulfilled before Jesus Christ will return.

God Has 3 -1/2 Years Of Destruction

a) God's Wrath - In Revelation 16:1-21 it says *"1 And I heard a great voice out of the temple saying to the seven angels, Go your ways, and pour out the vials of the wrath of God upon the earth. 2 And the first went, and poured out his vial upon the earth; and there fell a noisome and grievous sore upon the men which had the mark of the beast, and upon them which worshipped his image. 3 And the second angel poured out his vial upon the sea; and it became as the blood of a dead man; and every living soul died in the sea. 4 And the third angel poured out his vial upon the rivers and fountains of waters; and they became blood. 5 And I heard the angel of the waters say, Thou art righteous, O Lord,which art, and wast, and shalt be, because thou hast judged thus. 6 For they have shed the blood of saints and prophets, and thou hast given them blood to drink; for they are worthy. 7 And I heard another out of the altar say, Even so, Lord God Almighty, true and righteous are thy judgments. 8 And the fourth angel poured out his vial upon the sun; and power was given unto him to scorch men with fire. 9 And men were scorched with great heat, and blasphemed the name of God, which hath power over these plagues:and they repented not to give him glory. 10 And the fifth angel poured out his vial upon the seat of the beast; and his kingdom was full of darkness; and they gnawed their tongues for pain, 11 And blasphemed the God of heaven because of their pains and their sores, and repented not of their deeds. 12 And the sixth angel poured out his vial upon the great river Euphrates; and the water thereof was dried up, that the way of the kings of the east might be prepared. 13 And I saw three unclean spirits like frogs come out of the mouth of the dragon, and out of the mouth of the beast, and out of the mouth of the false prophet. 14 For they* are the spirits of devils, working miracles, which go forth unto the kings of the earth and of the whole world, to gather them to the battle of that great day of God Almighty. 15 Behold, I come as a thief. Blessed is he that watcheth, and keepeth his garments, lest he walk naked, and they see his shame. 16 And he gathered them together into a place called in the Hebrew tongue Armageddon. 17 And the seventh angel poured out his vial into the air; and there came a great voice out of the temple of heaven, from the throne, saying, It is done. 18 And there were voices, and thunders, and lightnings; and there was a great earthquake, such as was not since men were upon the earth, so mighty an earthquake, and so great. 19 And the great city was divided into three parts, and the cities of the nations fell: and great Babylon came in remembrance before God, to give unto her the cup of the wine of the fierceness of his wrath. 20 And every island fled away, and the mountains were not found. 21 And there fell upon men a great hail out of heaven, every stone about the weight of a talent: and men blasphemed God because of the plague of the hail; for the plague thereof was exceeding great."

b) **Satan's Wrath** - In Revelation 13:3-5, 15-18 it says "3 And I saw one of his heads as it were wounded to death; and his deadly wound was healed: and all the world wondered after the beast. 4 And they worshipped the dragon which gave power unto the beast: and they worshipped the beast, saying, Who is like unto the beast? who is able to make war with him? 5 And there was given unto him a mouth speaking great things and blasphemies; and power was given unto him to continue forty and two months. 15 And he had power to give life unto the image of the beast, that the image of the beast should both speak, and cause that as many as would not worship the image of the beast should be killed. 16 And he causeth all, both small and great, rich and poor, free and bond, to receive a mark in their right hand, or in their foreheads: 17 And that no man *might buy or sell, save he that had the mark, or the name of the beast, or the number of his name. 18 Here is wisdom. Let him that hath understanding count the number of the beast: for it is the number of a man; and his number is Six hundred threescore and six."* The Antichrist will have 3 -1/2 years of destruction.

We Have The Seal Of God In Our Forehead

a) God's People - In Revelation 9:1-4 it says *"1 And the fifth angel sounded, and I saw a star fall from heaven unto the earth: and to him was given the key of the bottomless pit. 2 And he opened the bottomless pit; and there arose a smoke out of the pit, as the smoke of a great furnace; and the sun and the air were darkened by reason of the smoke of the pit. 3 And there came out of the smoke locusts upon the earth: and unto them was given power, as the scorpions of the earth have power. 4 And it was commanded them that they should not hurt the grass of the earth, neither any green thing, neither any tree; but only those men which have not the seal of God in their foreheads."*

And in Revelation 7:1-4 it says *"1 And after these things I saw four angels standing on the four corners of the earth, holding the four winds of the earth, that the wind should not blow on the earth, nor on the sea, nor on any tree. 2 And I saw another angel ascending from the east, having the seal of the living God: and he cried with a loud voice to the four angels, to whom it was given to hurt the earth and the sea, 3 Saying, Hurt not the earth, neither the sea, nor the trees, till we have sealed the servants of our God in their foreheads. 4 And I heard the number of them which were sealed: and there were sealed an hundred and forty and four thousand of all the tribes of the children of Israel."*

b) Satan's People - In Revelation 13:15-18 it says *"15 And he had power to give life unto the image of the beast, that the* *image of the beast should both speak, and cause that as many as would not worship the image of the beast should be killed. 16 And he causeth all, both small and great, rich and poor, free and bond, to receive a mark in their right hand, or in their foreheads: 17 And that no man might buy or sell, save he that had the mark, or the name of the beast, or the number of his name. 18 Here is wisdom. Let him that hath understanding count the number of the beast: for it is the number of a man;and his number is Six hundred threescore and six."* This passage shows how Satan will try to get everyone to receive the mark of the beast.

CHAPTER 7

God's Holy Angels

But to which of the angels said he at any time, Sit on my right hand, until I make thine enemies thy footstool? Are they not all ministering spirits, sent forth to minister for them who shall be heirs of salvation? Hebrews 1:13-14

In this chapter we will show how God uses His angels.

Angels Protect What Is God's

In the book of Genesis, after man had sinned and had to be removed from the garden of Eden, God used his angels to protect the tree of life. In Genesis 3:20-24 it says *"20 And Adam called his wife's name Eve; because she was the mother of all living. 21 Unto Adam also and to his wife did the LORD God make coats of skins, and clothed them. 22 And the LORD God said, Behold, the man is become as one of us, to know good and evil: and now, lest he put forth his hand, and take also of the tree of life, and eat, and live for ever: 23 Therefore the LORD God sent him forth from the garden of Eden, to till the ground from whence he was taken. 24 So he drove out the man; and he placed at the east of the garden of Eden Cherubims, and a flaming sword which turned every way, to keep the way of the tree of life."* In Psalm 34:7 it says *"The angel of the LORD encampeth round about them that fear him, and delivereth them."* This scripture shows that God uses His holy angels to protect his people. In Matthew chapter 26 it shows us that Jesus could have prayed to the Father for more than twelve legions of angels. In Matthew 26:49-56 it says *"49 And forthwith he came to Jesus, and said, Hail, master; and kissed him. 50 And Jesus said unto him, Friend,wherefore art thou come? Then came they, and laid hands on Jesus, and took him. 51 And, behold, one of them which were with Jesus stretched out his hand, and drew his sword, and struck a servant of the high priest's, and smote off his ear. 52 Then said Jesus unto him, Put up again thy sword into his place: for all they that take the sword shall perish with the sword. 53 Thinkest thou that I cannot now pray to my Father, and he shall presently give me more than twelve legions of angels? 54 But how then shall the scriptures be fulfilled, that thus it must be? 55 In that same hour said Jesus to the multitudes, Are ye come out as against a thief with swords and staves for to take me? I sat daily with you teaching in the temple, and ye laid no hold on me. 56 But all this was done, that the scriptures of the prophets might be fulfilled. Then all the disciples forsook him, and fled."*

Angels Deliver God's People From Evil

In the book of Acts we see how God's holy angels delivered the apostle Peter from prison. In Acts 12:1-17 it says *"1 Now about that time Herod the king stretched forth his hands to vex certain of the church. 2 And he killed James the brother of John with the sword. 3 And because he saw it pleased the Jews, he proceeded further to take Peter also. (Then were the days of unleavened bread.) 4 And when he had apprehended him, he put him in prison, and delivered him to four quaternions of soldiers to keep him; intending after Easter to bring him forth to the people. 5 Peter therefore was kept in prison: but prayer was made without ceasing of the church unto God for him. 6*

And when Herod would have brought him forth, the same night Peter was sleeping between two soldiers, bound with two chains: and the keepers before the door kept the prison. 7 And, behold, the angel of the Lord came upon him, and a light shined in the prison: and he smote Peter on the side, and raised him up, saying, Arise up quickly. And his chains fell off from his hands. 8 And the angel said unto him, Gird thyself, and bind on thy sandals. And so he did. And he saith unto him, Cast thy garment about thee, and follow me. 9 And he went out, and followed him; and wist not that it was true which was done by the angel; but thought he saw a vision. 10 When they were past the first and the second ward, they came unto the iron gate that leadeth unto the city; which opened to them of his own accord: and they went out, and passed on through one street; and forthwith the angel departed from him. 11 And when Peter was come to himself, he said, Now I know of a surety, that the Lord hath sent his angel, and hath delivered me out of the hand of Herod, and from all the expectation of the people of the Jews. 12 And when he had considered the thing, he came to the house of Mary the mother of John, whose surname was Mark; where many were gathered together praying. 13 And as Peter knocked at the door of the gate, a damsel came to hearken, named Rhoda. 14 And when she knew Peter's voice, she opened not the gate for gladness, but ran in, and told how Peter stood before the gate. 15 And they said unto her, Thou art mad. But she constantly affirmed that it was even so. Then said they, It is his angel. 16 But Peter continued knocking: and when they had opened the door, and saw him, they were astonished. 17 But he, beckoning unto them with the hand to hold their peace, declared unto them how the Lord had brought him out of the prison. And he said, Go shew these things unto James, and to the brethren. And he departed, and went into another place."
Even the apostle Peter thought he saw a vision as the angel of God supernaturally delivered him from prison.

In Daniel chapter 6 we see another miracle when God's angels delivered Daniel from the lion's den. In Daniel 6:19-24 it says *"19 Then the king arose very early in the morning, and went in haste unto the den of lions. 20 And when he came to the den, he cried with a lamentable voice unto Daniel: and the king spake and said to Daniel, O Daniel, servant of the living God, is thy God, whom thou servest continually, able to deliver thee from the lions? 21 Then said Daniel unto the king, O king, live for ever. 22 My God hath sent his angel, and hath shut the lions' mouths, that they have not hurt me: forasmuch as before him innocency was found in me; and also before thee, O king, have I done no hurt. 23 Then was the king exceeding glad for him, and commanded that they should take Daniel up out of the den. So Daniel was taken up out of the den, and no manner of hurt was found upon him, because he believed in his God. 24 And the king commanded, and they brought those men which had accused Daniel, and they cast them into the den of lions, them, their children, and their wives; and the lions had the mastery of them, and brake all their bones in pieces or ever they came at the bottom of the den."*

In Acts chapter 5 the Lord sent His angel and delivered the apostles from prison and told them to continue to speak to the people in the temple about *"all the words of this life"*. In Acts 5:17-25 it says *"17 Then the high priest rose up, and all they that were with him, (which is the sect of the Sadducees,) and were filled with indignation, 18 And laid their hands on the apostles, and put them in the common prison. 19 But the angel of the Lord by night opened the prison doors, and brought them forth, and said, 20 Go, stand and speak in the temple to the people all the words of this life. 21 And when they heard that, they entered into the temple early in the morning, and taught. But the high priest came, and they that were with him, and called the council together, and all the senate of the children of Israel, and sent to the prison to have them brought. 22 But when the officers came, and found them not in the prison, they returned, and told, 23 Saying, The prison truly found we shut with all safety, and the keepers standing without before the doors: but when we had opened, we found no man within. 24 Now when the high priest and the captain of the temple and the chief priests heard these things, they doubted of them whereunto this would grow. 25 Then came one and told them, saying, Behold, the men whom ye put in prison are standing in the temple, and teaching the people."* We see not only did God deliver the apostles, but while the religious leaders were trying to bring the apostles before the council, the apostles were teaching in the temple.

In Genesis chapter 19 we see how God sent His angels to deliver Lot and his family from Sodom and Gomorrah. In Genesis 19:1-29 it says *"1 And there came two angels to Sodom at even; and Lot sat in the gate of Sodom: and Lot seeing them rose up to meet them; and he bowed himself with his face toward the ground; 2 And he said, Behold now, my lords, turn in, I pray you, into your servant's house, and tarry all night, and wash your feet, and ye shall rise up early, and go on your ways. And they said, Nay; but we will abide in the street all night. 3 And he pressed upon them greatly; and they turned in unto him, and entered into his house; and he made them a feast, and did bake unleavened bread, and they did eat. 4 But before they lay down, the men of the city, even the men of Sodom, compassed the house round, both old and young, all the people from every quarter: 5 And they called unto Lot, and said unto him, Where are the men which came in to thee this night? bring them out unto us, that we may know them. 6 And Lot went out at the door unto them, and shut the door after him, 7 And said, I pray you, brethren, do not so wickedly. 8 Behold now, I have two daughters which have not known man; let me, I pray you, bring them out unto you, and do ye to them as is good in your eyes: only unto these men do nothing; for therefore came they under the shadow of my roof. 9 And they said, Stand back. And they said again, This one fellow came in to sojourn, and he will needs be a judge: now will we deal worse with thee, than with them. And they pressed sore upon the man, even Lot, and came near to break the door. 10 But the men put forth their hand, and pulled Lot into the house to them, and shut to the door. 11 And they smote the men that were at the door of the house with blindness, both small and great: so that they wearied themselves to find the door. 12 And the men said unto Lot, Hast thou here any besides? son in law, and thy sons, and thy daughters, and whatsoever thou hast in the city, bring them out of this place: 13 For we will destroy this place, because the cry of them is waxen great before the face of the LORD; and the LORD hath sent us to destroy it. 14 And Lot went out, and spake unto his sons in law, which married his daughters, and said, Up, get you out of this place; for the LORD will destroy this city. But he seemed as one that mocked unto his sons in law. 15 And when the morning arose, then the angels hastened Lot, saying, Arise, take thy wife, and thy two daughters, which are here; lest thou be consumed in the iniquity of the city. 16 And while he lingered, the men laid hold upon his hand, and upon the hand of his wife, and upon the hand of his two daughters; the LORD being merciful unto him: and they brought him forth, and set him without the city. 17 And it came to pass, when they had brought them forth abroad, that he said, Escape for thy life; look not behind thee, neither stay thou in all the plain; escape to the mountain, lest thou be consumed. 18 And Lot said unto them, Oh, not so, my Lord: 19 Behold now, thy servant hath found grace in thy sight, and thou hast magnified thy mercy, which thou hast shewed unto me in saving my life; and I cannot escape to the mountain, lest some evil take me, and I die: 20 Behold now, this city is near to flee unto, and it is a little one: Oh, let me escape thither, (is it not a little one?) and my soul shall live. 21 And he said unto him, See, I have accepted thee concerning this thing also, that I will not overthrow this city, for the which thou hast spoken. 22 Haste thee, escape thither; for I cannot do any thing till thou be come thither. Therefore the name of the city was called Zoar. 23 The sun was risen upon the earth when Lot entered into Zoar. 24 Then the LORD rained upon Sodom and upon Gomorrah brimstone and fire from the LORD out of heaven; 25 And he overthrew those cities, and all the plain, and all the inhabitants of the cities, and that which grew upon the ground. 26 But his wife looked back from behind him, and she became a pillar of salt. 27 And Abraham gat up early in the morning to the place where he stood before the LORD: 28 And he looked toward Sodom and Gomorrah, and toward all the land of the plain, and beheld, and, lo, the smoke of the country went up as the smoke of a furnace. 29 And it came to pass, when God destroyed the cities of the plain, that God remembered Abraham, and sent Lot out of the midst of the overthrow, when he overthrew the cities in the which Lot dwelt."* Notice verse 22 which states*" Haste thee, escape thither; for I cannot do any thing till thou be come thither. Therefore the name of the city was called Zoar."* God delayed destroying Sodom and Gomorrah until Lot and family entered the city Zoar.

God still uses His angels to protect His people today. I would like to share two testimonies of how God used His holy angels to protect me. In the 1980's in Seattle, Washington, I was invited to eat Thanksgiving dinner with a Christian family. That night, after dinner, as I was driving home, I approached an intersection that led to a very busy street. Suddenly, about a block before this intersection, the Spirit of the Lord came upon me and I pulled over and began to pray in Tongues. A few seconds after I began to pray in Tongues, a car came speeding down the street I was about to turn onto and smashed into a steel pole at the same intersection that I would have been at if the Lord had not stopped me to pray. Praise be to Jesus Christ!

My second testimony showing how God still uses His angels to protect His people today occurred in December 1988, in Redmond, Washington. My wife and I were on our way home at night. Our car was in the auto repair shop being fixed. We were driving a very small loaner car. We were exiting a highway which intersected with a main thoroughfare that runs through the cities of Redmond and Bellevue. As we went through the intersection a driver on the cross street ran the red light and pulled his vehicle in front of ours. Since we were exiting the freeway we were driving at a fairly fast rate of speed, and even though I tried, there was nothing I could do to avoid hitting this vehicle. The car we were in was destroyed. However, we give God all the Praise for His protection. My wife and I were able to walk away from this accident with very minor scrapes. The driver of the vehicle we hit was not hurt at all. We took a picture of the car we were driving after the accident, and we knew God's holy angels protected us because from the damage to the car it looked like a fatal accident had taken place.

Angels Will Only Confirm The Word Of God

In Galatians, the apostle Paul tells us if we or an angel preach another gospel let him be accursed. In Galatians 1:8-10 it says *"8 But though we, or an angel from heaven, preach any other gospel unto you than that which we have preached unto you, let him be accursed. 9 As we said before, so say I now again, If any man preach any other gospel unto you than that ye have received, let him be accursed. 10 For do I now persuade men, or God? or do I seek to please men? for if I yet pleased men, I should not be the servant of Christ."* The apostle Paul was saying that the angels that preach another gospel are fallen angels, or demons. The angels of God will only confirm the Word of God.

Angels Are Not To Be Worshipped

In Revelation, the apostle John fell at the feet of the angel to worship him and the angel corrected him and told him to worship God. In Revelation 19:10 it says *"And I fell at his feet to worship him. And he said unto me, See thou do it not: I am thy fellowservant, and of thy brethren that have the testimony of Jesus: worship God: for the testimony of Jesus is the spirit of prophecy."* And in Revelation 22:8-9 it says *"8 And I John saw these things, and heard them. And when I had heard and seen, I fell down to worship before the feet of the angel which shewed me these things. 9 Then saith he unto me, See thou do it not: for I am thy fellowservant, and of thy brethren the prophets, and of them which keep the sayings of this book: worship God."*

Angels Interpret Dreams Or Visions Of God

The first thing I would like to say is that every dream or vision is not from God. We can see some examples of this from Jeremiah 23:32 and Ezekiel 13:16. In Jeremiah 23:32 it says *"Behold, I am against them that prophesy false dreams, saith the LORD, and do tell them, and cause my people to err by their lies, and by their lightness; yet I sent them not, nor commanded them: therefore they shall not profit this people at all, saith the LORD."* Also, in Ezekiel 13:16 it says *"To wit, the prophets of Israel which prophesy concerning Jerusalem, and which see visions of peace for her, and there is no peace, saith the Lord GOD."*

We see from the scriptures that God often used His angels to interpret dreams and visions of God. God used His angels to interpret a dream that Daniel had. In Daniel 8:15-27 it says

"15 And it came to pass, when I, even I Daniel, had seen the vision, and sought for the meaning, then, behold, there stood before me as the appearance of a man. 16 And I heard a man's voice between the banks of Ulai, which called, and said, Gabriel, make this man to understand the vision. 17 So he came near where I stood: and when he came, I was afraid, and fell upon my face: but he said unto me, Understand, O son of man: for at the time of the end shall be the vision. 18 Now as he was speaking with me, I was in a deep sleep on my face toward the ground: but he touched me, and set me upright. 19 And he said, Behold, I will make thee know what shall be in the last end of the indignation: for at the time appointed the end shall be. 20 The ram which thou sawest having two horns are the kings of Media and Persia. 21 And the rough goat is the king of Grecia: and the great horn that is between his eyes is the first king. 22 Now that being broken, whereas four stood up for it, four kingdoms shall stand up out of the nation, but not in his power. 23 And in the latter time of their kingdom, when the transgressors are come to the full, a king of fierce countenance, and understanding dark sentences, shall stand up. 24 And his power shall be mighty, but not by his own power: and he shall destroy wonderfully, and shall prosper, and practise, and shall destroy the mighty and the holy people. 25 And through his policy also he shall cause craft to prosper in his hand; and he shall magnify himself in his heart, and by peace shall destroy many: he shall also stand up against the Prince of princes; but he shall be broken without hand. 26 And the vision of the evening and the morning which was told is true: wherefore shut thou up the vision; for it shall be for many days. 27 And I Daniel fainted, and was sick certain days; afterward I rose up, and did the king's business; and I was astonished at the vision, but none understood it."

In Revelation chapter 17 one of God's angels told John the meaning of his vision. In Revelation 17:7-18 it says *"7 And the angel said unto me, Wherefore didst thou marvel? I will tell thee the mystery of the woman, and of the beast that carrieth her, which hath the seven heads and ten horns. 8 The beast that thou sawest was, and is not; and shall ascend out of the bottomless pit, and go into perdition: and they that dwell on the earth shall wonder, whose names were not written in the book of life from the foundation of the world, when they behold the beast that was, and is not, and yet is. 9 And here is the mind which hath wisdom. The seven heads are seven mountains, on which the woman sitteth. 10 And there are seven kings: five are fallen, and one is, and the other is not yet come; and when he cometh, he must continue a short space. 11 And the beast that was, and is not, even he is the eighth, and is of the seven, and goeth into perdition. 12 And the ten horns which thou sawest are ten kings, which have received no kingdom as yet; but receive power as kings one hour with the beast. 13 These have one mind, and shall give their power and strength unto the beast. 14 These shall make war with the Lamb, and the Lamb shall overcome them: for he is Lord of lords, and King of kings: and they that are with him are called, and chosen, and faithful. 15 And he saith unto me, The waters which thou sawest, where the whore sitteth, are peoples, and multitudes, and nations, and tongues. 16 And the ten horns which thou sawest upon the beast, these shall hate the whore, and shall make her desolate and naked, and shall eat her flesh, and burn her with fire. 17 For God hath put in their hearts to fulfil his will, and to agree, and give their kingdom unto the beast, until the words of God shall be fulfilled. 18 And the woman which thou sawest is that great city, which reigneth over the kings of the earth."*

Angels Sometimes Appear As Men

In Daniel chapter 8 the angel Gabriel had the appearance of a man. In Daniel 8:15-16 it says *"15 And it came to pass, when I, even I Daniel, had seen the vision, and sought for the meaning, then, behold, there stood before me as the appearance of a man. 16 And I heard a man's voice between the banks of Ulai, which called, and said, Gabriel, make this man to understand the vision."* And in the gospel of Luke the same angel Gabriel appeared to Zacharias the priest. In Luke 1:11-13, 19 it says *"11 And there appeared unto him an angel of the Lord standing on the right side of the altar of incense. 12 And when Zacharias saw him, he was troubled, and fear fell upon him. 13 But the angel said unto him, Fear not, Zacharias: for thy prayer is heard; and thy wife Elisabeth shall bear thee a son, and thou shalt call his name John....19 And the angel answering said unto him, I am Gabriel, that stand in the presence of God; and am sent to speak unto thee, and to shew thee these glad tidings."*

Angels Carry Or Transport God's Message

God uses His angels to send his people messages from Him. In Daniel 9:20-23 it says *"20 And whiles I was speaking, and praying, and confessing my sin and the sin of my people Israel, and presenting my supplication before the LORD my God for the holy mountain of my God; 21 Yea, whiles I was speaking in prayer, even the man Gabriel, whom I had seen in the vision at the beginning, being caused to fly swiftly, touched me about the time of the evening oblation. 22 And he informed me, and talked with me, and said, O Daniel, I am now come forth to give thee skill and understanding. 23 At the beginning of thy supplications the commandment came forth, and I am come to shew thee; for thou art greatly beloved: therefore understand the matter, and consider the vision."*

God sent His angel to tell Zacharias that his wife would have a child. In Luke 1:18-25 it says *"18 And Zacharias said unto the angel, Whereby shall I know this? for I am an old man, and my wife well stricken in years. 19 And the angel answering said unto him, I am Gabriel, that stand in the presence of God; and am sent to speak unto thee, and to shew thee these glad tidings. 20 And, behold, thou shalt be dumb, and not able to speak, until the day that these things shall be performed, because thou believest not my words, which shall be fulfilled in their season. 21 And the people waited for Zacharias, and marvelled that he tarried so long in the temple. 22 And when he came out, he could not speak unto them: and they perceived that he had seen a vision in the temple: for he beckoned unto them, and remained speechless. 23 And it came to pass, that, as soon as the days of his ministration were accomplished, he departed to his own house. 24 And after those days his wife Elisabeth conceived, and hid herself five months, saying, 25 Thus hath the Lord dealt with me in the days wherein he looked on me, to take away my reproach among men."*

Angels Inflict Divine Penalties

God uses his angels to destroy those who sinned against him. In I Chronicles 21:14-16,27 it says *"14 So the LORD sent pestilence upon Israel: and there fell of Israel seventy thousand men. 15 And God sent an angel unto Jerusalem to destroy it: and as he was destroying, the LORD beheld, and he repented him of the evil, and said to the angel that destroyed, It is enough, stay now thine hand. And the angel of the LORD stood by the threshingfloor of Ornan the Jebusite. 16 And David lifted up his eyes, and saw the angel of the LORD stand between the earth and the heaven, having a drawn sword in his hand stretched out over Jerusalem. Then David and the elders of Israel, who were clothed in sackcloth, fell upon their faces... 27 And the LORD commanded the angel; and he put up his sword again into the sheath thereof."*

In Acts chapter 12 God used His angel to smite Herod because he gave not God the glory. In Acts 12:21-23 it says *"21 And* upon a set day Herod, arrayed in royal apparel, sat upon his throne, and made an oration unto them. 22 And the people gave a shout, saying, It is the voice of a god, and not of a man. 23 And immediately the angel of the Lord smote him, because he gave not God the glory: and he was eaten of worms, and gave up the ghost."

Angels Are Ministering Spirits

God used His angel to minister to the prophet Elijah. In I Kings 19:5-7 it says *"5 And as he lay and slept under a juniper tree, behold, then an angel touched him, and said unto him, Arise and eat. 6 And he looked, and, behold, there was a cake baken on the coals, and a cruse of water at his head. And he did eat and drink, and laid him down again. 7 And the angel of the LORD came again the second time, and touched him, and said, Arise and eat; because the journey is too great for thee."* In Acts chapter 8 the angel led the evangelist Philip to an Ethiopian eunuch who through the preaching of Jesus was saved. In Acts 8:26 it says *" 26 And the angel of the Lord spake unto Philip, saying, Arise, and go toward the south unto the way that goeth down from Jerusalem unto Gaza, which is desert."*

Angels Sound The Trumpets Of God's Judgement

God uses His angels to sound the trumpets of judgement on the earth. In Revelation 8:6-13 it says *"6 And the seven angels which had the seven trumpets prepared themselves to sound. 7 The first angel sounded, and there followed hail and fire mingled with blood, and they were cast upon the earth: and the third part of trees was burnt up, and all green grass was burnt up. 8 And the second angel sounded, and as it were a great mountain burning with fire was cast into the sea: and the third part of the sea became blood; 9 And the third part of the creatures which were in the sea, and had life, died; and the third part of the ships were destroyed. 10 And the third angel sounded, and there fell a great star from heaven, burning as it were a lamp, and it fell upon the third part of the rivers, and upon the fountains of waters; 11 And the name of the star is called Wormwood: and the third part of the waters became wormwood; and many men died of the waters, because they were made bitter. 12 And the fourth angel sounded, and the third part of the sun was smitten, and the third part of the moon, and the third part of the stars; so as the third part of them was darkened, and the day shone not for a third part of it, and the night likewise. 13 And I beheld, and heard an angel flying through the midst of heaven, saying with a loud voice, Woe, woe, woe, to the inhabiters of the earth by reason of the other voices of the trumpet of the three angels, which are yet to sound!"*

CHAPTER 8

Why God Must Judge
The Church

---

*For the time is come that judgment must begin at the
house of God: and if it first begin at us, what shall the
end be of them that obey not the gospel of God? And if
the righteous scarcely be saved, where shall the
ungodly and the sinner appear?I Peter 4:17-18*

God must judge the church because of the sins of church
leadership and the sins of the Christians.

Sins Of The Church Leadership

Many Church Leaders Have Compromised God's Word

The apostle Paul told us in the latter time some would depart
from the faith and be deceived by seducing spirits and doctrine
of devils. These people were once in the faith but were
deceived by Satan. In I Timothy 4:1 it says *"Now the Spirit
speaketh expressly, that in the latter times some shall depart
from the faith, giving heed to seducing spirits, and doctrines of
devils;"* The apostle Paul gave us an example of two people,

Hymenaeus and Alexander, who were deceived by Satan. In I Timothy 1:18-20 it says *"18 This charge I commit unto thee, son Timothy, according to the prophecies which went before on thee, that thou by them mightest war a good warfare; 19 Holding faith, and a good conscience; which some having put away concerning faith have made shipwreck: 20 Of whom is Hymenaeus and Alexander; whom I have delivered unto Satan, that they may learn not to blaspheme."* In II Timothy he tells how both of them did evil in the sight of God. In II Timothy 2:17-18 it says *"17 And their word will eat as doth a canker: of whom is Hymenaeus and Philetus; 18 Who concerning the truth have erred, saying that the resurrection is past already; and overthrow the faith of some."* And in II Timothy 4:14 it says *"14 Alexander the coppersmith did me much evil: the Lord reward him according to his works:"*

Many Church Leaders Are Men Pleasers

Many church leaders are focused on pleasing their congregation instead of pleasing God. They attract people to their churches with "barbecues," Christmas and Easter plays and other social activities. They keep the children busy with expensive Sunday School toys and trinkets. They spend thousands of dollars on elaborate entertainment systems to satisfy the congregation's desire for music. They ignore the teenagers and adults who date and fornicate. They perform marriage ceremonies uniting church or non-church members, saved or not. And at the same time, these pastors ignore the spiritual pits that their church members are in and let their souls go to hell.

Notice what the apostle Paul says in Galatians 1:10 about people who seek to please men instead of God. In Galatians 1:10 it says *" For do I now persuade men, or God? or do I seek to please men? for if I yet pleased men, I should not be the servant of Christ."* The apostle Paul tells us how true ministers should preach. In I Thessalonians 2:4-5 it says *"4 But as we were allowed of God to be put in trust with the gospel, even so we speak; not as pleasing men, but God, which trieth our hearts. 5 For neither at any time used we flattering words, as ye know, nor a cloke of covetousness; God is witness:"*

Many Church Leaders Are Preaching Doctrines Of Men

The apostle Paul told us that Jewish fables and commandments of men turn us from the truth. In Titus 1:14 it says *"Not giving heed to Jewish fables, and commandments of men, that turn from the truth."* Jesus Christ spoke concerning this very thing in his day about the doctrine of the Pharisees and of the Sadducees. In Matthew 16:6-12 it says *"6 Then Jesus said unto them, Take heed and beware of the leaven of the Pharisees and of the Sadducees. 7 And they reasoned among themselves, saying, It is because we have taken no bread. 8 Which when Jesus perceived, he said unto them, O ye of little faith, why reason ye among yourselves, because ye have brought no bread? 9 Do ye not yet understand, neither remember the five loaves of the five thousand, and how many baskets ye took up? 10 Neither the seven loaves of the four thousand, and how many baskets ye took up? 11 How is it that ye do not understand that I spake it not to you concerning bread, that ye should beware of the leaven of the Pharisees and of the Sadducees? 12 Then understood they how that he bade them not beware of the leaven of bread, but of the doctrine of the Pharisees and of the Sadducees."*

One area where many are preaching a doctrine of men is concerning the Holy Ghost. They say that everyone who is saved has already received the Holy Ghost. But this is not true. In Acts chapter 19 the apostle Paul tells us the truth about the Baptism in the Holy Ghost. In Acts 19:1-7 it says *"1 And it came to pass, that, while Apollos was at Corinth, Paul having passed through the upper coasts came to Ephesus: and finding certain disciples, 2 He said unto them, Have ye received the Holy Ghost since ye believed? And they said unto him, We have not so much as heard whether there be any Holy Ghost. 3 And he said unto them, Unto what then were ye baptized? And they said, Unto John's baptism. 4 Then said Paul, John verily baptized with the baptism of repentance, saying unto the people, that they should believe on him which should come after him, that is, on Christ Jesus. 5 When they heard this, they were baptized in the name of the Lord Jesus. 6 And when Paul had laid his hands upon them, the Holy Ghost came on them; and they spake with tongues, and prophesied. 7 And all the men were about twelve."* This scripture clearly states that they were saved and had not received the Baptism in the Holy Ghost. It shows that the Baptism in the Holy Ghost is an additional step that we need to take after we are saved. We will continue to share more about this in Chapter 10 "What Can A Christian Do?"

Many Ministers Have Rejected The Other Gifts Of Ministry In The Church

In Ephesians chapter 4 the apostle Paul discusses the five gifts of ministry in the church. Ephesians 4:11-16 says *"11 And he gave some, apostles; and some, prophets; and some, evangelists; and some, pastors and teachers; 12 For the perfecting of the saints, for the work of the ministry, for the edifying of the body of Christ: 13 Till we all come in the unity of the faith, and of the knowledge of the Son of God, unto a perfect man, unto the measure of the stature of the fulness of Christ: 14 That we henceforth be no more children, tossed to and fro, and carried about with every wind of doctrine, by the sleight of men, and cunning craftiness, whereby they lie in wait to deceive; 15 But speaking the truth in love, may grow up into him in all things, which is the head, even Christ: 16 From whom the whole body fitly joined together and compacted by that which every joint supplieth, according to the effectual working in the measure of every part, maketh increase of the body unto the edifying of itself in love."*

Many ministers today have rejected the apostle and prophet ministry and this has caused the church to be in a bad state today. True apostles and prophets are not those that have been given these titles by men. True apostles and prophets of God are those that have been anointed by the Holy Ghost and that have messages of power and hope and repentance for the body of Christ. Until all five gifts of ministry are in full operation in the church, the church will never come to it's fulness as the body of Jesus Christ.

Many Church Leaders Have Built Their Own Kingdoms And Not The Kingdom Of God

Many ministers have built their own ministries, and in the time of testing these ministries will not stand because they were not built on the Rock Jesus Christ. In Matthew 7:24-27 it says *"24 Therefore whosoever heareth these sayings of mine, and doeth them, I will liken him unto a wise man, which built his house upon a rock: 25 And the rain descended, and the floods came, and the winds blew, and beat upon that house; and it fell not: for it was founded upon a rock. 26 And every one that heareth these sayings of mine, and doeth them not, shall be likened unto a foolish man, which built his house upon the sand: 27 And the rain descended, and the floods came, and the winds blew, and beat upon that house; and it fell: and great was the fall of it."* In the book of Hebrews God speaks of a great shaking in the earth and heaven. In Hebrews 12:25-27 it says *"25 See that ye refuse not him that speaketh. For if they escaped not who refused him that spake on earth, much more shall not we escape, if we turn away from him that speaketh from heaven: 26 Whose voice then shook the earth: but now he hath promised, saying, Yet once more I shake not the earth only, but also heaven. 27 And this word, Yet once more, signifieth the removing of those things that are shaken, as of things that are made, that those things which cannot be shaken may remain."*

Many Ministers Have Given Glory To Men When The Glory Should Be To Jesus Christ

The apostle Paul was very humble and let everybody know that it is Jesus Christ who must get all the glory for what is done on this earth. In I Corinthians 1:18-31 it says *"18 For the preaching of the cross is to them that perish foolishness; but unto us which are saved it is the power of God. 19 For it is written, I will destroy the wisdom of the wise, and will bring to nothing the understanding of the prudent. 20 Where is the wise? where is the scribe? where is the disputer of this world? hath not God made foolish the wisdom of this world? 21 For after that in the wisdom of God the world by wisdom knew not God, it pleased God by the foolishness of preaching to save them that believe. 22 For the Jews require a sign, and the Greeks seek after wisdom: 23 But we preach Christ crucified, unto the Jews a stumblingblock, and unto the Greeks foolishness; 24 But unto them which are called, both Jews and Greeks, Christ the power of God, and the wisdom of God. 25 Because the foolishness of God is wiser than men; and the weakness of God is stronger than men. 26 For ye see your calling, brethren, how that not many wise men after the flesh, not many mighty, not many noble, are called: 27 But God hath chosen the foolish things of the world to confound the wise; and God hath chosen the weak things of the world to confound the things which are mighty; 28 And base things of the world, and things which are despised, hath God chosen, yea, and things which are not, to bring to nought things that are: 29 That no flesh should glory in his presence. 30 But of him are ye in Christ Jesus, who of God is*

Page 124

made unto us wisdom, and righteousness, and sanctification, and redemption: 31 That, according as it is written, He that glorieth, let him glory in the Lord." Paul said also in I Corinthians 3:1-7 *"1 And I, brethren, could not speak unto you as unto spiritual, but as unto carnal, even as unto babes in Christ. 2 I have fed you with milk, and not with meat: for hitherto ye were not able to bear it, neither yet now are ye able. 3 For ye are yet carnal: for whereas there is among you envying, and strife, and divisions, are ye not carnal, and walk as men? 4 For while one saith, I am of Paul; and another, I am of Apollos; are ye not carnal? 5 Who then is Paul, and who is Apollos, but ministers by whom ye believed, even as the Lord gave to every man? 6 I have planted, Apollos watered; but God gave the increase. 7 So then neither is he that planteth any thing, neither he that watereth; but God that giveth the increase."*

Many Ministers Have Fed Themselves Instead Of Feeding God's People

The prophet Ezekiel spoke a powerful prophecy to those shepherds or pastors who were concerned about feeding themselves instead of feeding the flock. In Ezekiel 34:1-10 it says *"1 And the word of the LORD came unto me, saying, 2 Son of man, prophesy against the shepherds of Israel, prophesy, and say unto them, Thus saith the Lord GOD unto the shepherds; Woe be to the shepherds of Israel that do feed themselves! should not the shepherds feed the flocks? 3 Ye eat the fat, and ye clothe you with the wool, ye kill them that are fed: but ye feed not the flock. 4 The diseased have ye not strengthened, neither have ye healed that which was sick, neither have ye bound up that which was broken, neither have ye brought again that which was driven away, neither have ye sought that which was lost; but with force and with cruelty have ye ruled them. 5 And they were scattered, because there is no shepherd: and they became meat to all the beasts of the field, when they were scattered. 6 My sheep wandered through all the mountains, and upon every high hill: yea, my flock was scattered upon all the face of the earth, and none did search or seek after them. 7 Therefore, ye shepherds, hear the word of the LORD; 8 As I live, saith the Lord GOD, surely because my flock became a prey, and my flock became meat to every beast of the field, because there was no shepherd, neither did my shepherds search for my flock, but the shepherds fed themselves, and fed not my flock; 9 Therefore, O ye shepherds, hear the word of the LORD; 10 Thus saith the Lord GOD; Behold, I am against the shepherds; and I will require my flock at their hand, and cause them to cease from feeding the flock; neither shall the shepherds feed themselves any more; for I will deliver my flock from their mouth, that they may not be meat for them."* God's judgement came on these shepherds and they lost their flock.

The prophet Jeremiah had a similar message. In Jeremiah 10:21 it says *"21 For the pastors are become brutish, and have not sought the LORD: therefore they shall not prosper, and all their flocks shall be scattered."*

We can see examples of these scriptures being fulfilled today. Many ministers are concerned with accumulating worldly wealth and ignoring the spiritual needs of their flocks. God is destroying ministries that do not glorify Him.

Sins Of The Christians

Christians Are Unequally Yoked Together With Unbelievers

Many Christians today are imitating the world instead of being an example to the world. Instead of being a living holy example of God's power they are participating with the unsaved in the same sins. In II Corinthians chapter 6 Paul tells us not to be unequally yoked together with unbelievers. II Corinthians 6:14-18 says *"14 Be ye not unequally yoked together with unbelievers: for what fellowship hath righteousness with unrighteousness? and what communion hath light with darkness? 15 And what concord hath Christ with Belial? or what part hath he that believeth with an infidel? 16 And what agreement hath the temple of God with idols? for ye are the temple of the living God; as God hath said, I will dwell in them, and walk in them; and I will be their God, and they shall be my people. 17 Wherefore come out from among them, and be ye separate, saith the Lord, and touch not the unclean thing; and I will receive you, 18 And will be a Father unto you, and ye shall be my sons and daughters, saith the Lord Almighty."* In Ephesians chapter 5 Paul shows us another scripture about not being unequally yoked with unbelievers. In Ephesians 5:6-11 it says *"6 Let no man deceive you with vain words: for because of these things cometh the wrath of God upon the children of disobedience. 7 Be not ye therefore partakers with them. 8 For ye were sometimes darkness, but now are ye light in the Lord: walk as children of light: 9 (For the fruit of the Spirit is in all goodness and righteousness and truth;) 10 Proving what is acceptable unto the Lord. 11 And have no fellowship with the unfruitful works of darkness, but rather reprove them."*

Christians Are Not Students of the Word Of God

Many people who call themselves Christians are very ignorant of the faith that they say they believe in. In Hebrews chapter 5 we see a similar example in the Christians of that day. In Hebrews 5:11-13 it says *"11 Of whom we have many things to say, and hard to be uttered, seeing ye are dull of hearing. 12 For when for the time ye ought to be teachers, ye have need that one teach you again which be the first principles of the oracles of God; and are become such as have need of milk, and not of strong meat. 13 For every one that useth milk is unskilful in the word of righteousness: for he is a babe."* Notice verse 12 of this passage of scripture *"12 For when for the time ye ought to be teachers, ye have need that one teach you again which be the first principles of the oracles of God; and are become such as have need of milk, and not of strong meat."* They should have been teachers but were still babes in Christ. Many reading this book fit this same description. You have been in a church for many years yet you are still a babe when it comes to your relationship with Jesus Christ. You must repent immediately and rededicate your life to Jesus Christ and pray for wisdom in His Holy Word and spend time in the Holy Bible.

In Galatians chapter 1 Paul shows us another example of how quickly Christians can be deceived by not being students of the Word Of God. In Galatians 1:6-7 it says *"6 I marvel that ye are so soon removed from him that called you into the grace of Christ unto another gospel: 7 Which is not another; but there be some that trouble you, and would pervert the gospel of Christ."* Notice Paul marveled how soon they were removed to another gospel.

Christians Are Not Able To Discern Between Good And Evil

Many Christians today are not able to discern between good and evil. So many Christians are believing fables and not the truth of God's Holy Word. In II Timothy 4:3-4 it says *"For the time will come when they will not endure sound doctrine; but after their own lusts shall they heap to themselves teachers, having itching ears; And they shall turn away their ears from the truth, and shall be turned unto fables."*

Two examples of fables which many Christians are believing in are the Pre-Rapture or First Trumpet message (see Chapter 2 - Let No Man Deceive You) and the false teaching about the

Baptism in the Holy Ghost (see page 121 "Many Church Leaders Are Preaching Doctrines Of Men").

The apostle Peter shows the results of being deceived. In II Peter 2:17-22 it says *"17 These are wells without water, clouds that are carried with a tempest; to whom the mist of darkness is reserved for ever. 18 For when they speak great swelling words of vanity, they allure through the lusts of the flesh, through much wantonness, those that were clean escaped from them who live in error. 19 While they promise them liberty, they themselves are the servants of corruption: for of whom a man is overcome, of the same is he brought in bondage. 20 For if after they have escaped the pollutions of the world through the knowledge of the Lord and Saviour Jesus Christ, they are again entangled therein, and overcome, the latter end is worse with them than the beginning. 21 For it had been better for them not to have known the way of righteousness, than, after they have known it, to turn from the holy commandment delivered unto them. 22 But it is happened unto them according to the true proverb, The dog is turned to his own vomit again; and the sow that was washed to her wallowing in the mire."*

Many Christians Are Not Praying

Many Christians do not pray, and many of those who do pray do not wait for the answer from Jesus Christ. Notice what Jesus said to his disciples when he was praying at Gethsemane. Matthew 26:41 says *"Watch and pray, that ye enter not into temptation: the spirit indeed is willing, but the flesh is weak."* Also, in Luke 22:46 it says *"And said unto them, Why sleep ye? rise and pray, lest ye enter into temptation."* How can Christians have a relationship with Jesus Christ when they refuse to spend time with Him?

In chapter 10 we will discuss "What Can A Christian Do?" and how you can draw closer to the Lord Jesus Christ.

CHAPTER 9

Seventy Weeks

"Seventy weeks are determined upon thy people and upon thy holy city, to finish the transgression, and to make an end of sins, and to make reconciliation for iniquity, and to bring in everlasting righteousness, and to seal up the vision and prophecy, and to anoint the most Holy."
Daniel 9:24

This chapter explains the seventy weeks revealed through the angel Gabriel.

Daniel Visited By The Angel Gabriel

In Daniel chapter 9, the prophet Daniel is praying and confessing his sins and the sins of the people of Israel because of the seventy years of desolation which were prophesied by Jeremiah. The angel Gabriel came to Daniel. In Daniel 9:20-21 it says *"20 And whiles I was speaking, and praying, and confessing my sin and the sin of my people Israel, and presenting my supplication before the LORD my God for the holy mountain of my God; 21 Yea, whiles I was speaking in prayer, even the man Gabriel, whom I had seen in the vision at the beginning, being caused to fly swiftly, touched me about the time of the evening oblation."* Notice this is the same angel that visited the virgin Mary in Luke's gospel. In Luke 1:26-27 it says *"26 And in the sixth month the angel Gabriel was sent from God unto a city of Galilee, named Nazareth, 27 To a virgin espoused to a man whose name was Joseph, of the house of David; and the virgin's name was Mary."* The angel Gabriel also visited the prophet Daniel in chapter 8 of the book of Daniel. In Daniel 8:15-18 it says *"15 And it came to pass, when I, even I Daniel, had seen the vision, and sought for the meaning, then, behold, there stood before me as the appearance of a man. 16 And I heard a man's voice between the banks of Ulai, which called, and said, Gabriel, make this man to understand the vision. 17 So he came near where I stood: and when he came, I was afraid, and fell upon my face: but he said unto me, Understand, O son of man: for at the time of the end shall be the vision. 18 Now as he was speaking with me, I was in a deep sleep on my face toward the ground: but he touched me, and set me upright."*

The Angel Gabriel Came To Give The Prophet Daniel Understanding Of His Vision

In verse 21 *"Yea, whiles I was speaking in prayer, even the man Gabriel, whom I had seen in the vision at the beginning"* the prophet Daniel had a vision and the angel Gabriel came to give him understanding of the vision. In Daniel 9:22-23 it says *"22 And he informed me, and talked with me, and said, O Daniel, I am now come forth to give thee skill and understanding. 23 At the beginning of thy supplications the commandment came forth, and I am come to shew thee; for thou art greatly beloved: therefore understand the matter, and consider the vision."*

The Seventy Weeks Revealed
To The Prophet Daniel

In Daniel 9:24, the angel Gabriel speaks about a seventy week period of time. He says that during this time sin would end and everlasting righteousness would come. Daniel 9:24 says *"Seventy weeks are determined upon thy people and upon thy holy city, to finish the transgression, and to make an end of sins, and to make reconciliation for iniquity, and to bring in everlasting righteousness, and to seal up the vision and prophecy, and to anoint the most Holy."* From this passage of scripture we can see that the completion of the seventy weeks has not been fulfilled yet.

One Week Equals Seven Years Of Time

In the week of creation God rested on the seventh day which is the sabbath. In Genesis 2:1-3 it says *"1 Thus the heavens and the earth were finished, and all the host of them. 2 And on the seventh day God ended his work which he had made; and he rested on the seventh day from all his work which he had made. 3 And God blessed the seventh day, and sanctified it: because that in it he had rested from all his work which God created and made."*

Notice with the children of Israel, by calling an entire year a sabbath, that God related seven years to a week of time. In Leviticus 25:1-4 it says *"1 And the LORD spake unto Moses in mount Sinai, saying, 2 Speak unto the children of Israel, and say unto them, When ye come into the land which I give you, then shall the land keep a sabbath unto the LORD. 3 Six years thou shalt sow thy field, and six years thou shalt prune thy vineyard, and gather in the fruit thereof; 4 But in the seventh year shall be a sabbath of rest unto the land, a sabbath for the*

LORD: thou shalt neither sow thy field, nor prune thy vineyard."

Another confirmation is in Genesis 29:27 where Jacob refers to one week as seven years. In Genesis 29:27 it says *"Fulfil her week, and we will give thee this also for the service which thou shalt serve with me yet seven other years."*

Sixty-Nine Weeks Of The Seventy Weeks Have Been Fulfilled

In Daniel 9:25 Gabriel says *"Know therefore and understand, that from the going forth of the commandment to restore and to build Jerusalem unto the Messiah the Prince shall be seven weeks, and threescore and two weeks: the street shall be built again, and the wall, even in troublous times."* Notice that this scripture speaks of a period of sixty-nine weeks. Since one week equals seven years, sixty-nine weeks represents 483 years of time (69 x 7 = 483 years). But when did this 483 years start? The first part of Daniel 9:25 says *"Know therefore and understand, that from the going forth of the commandment to restore and to build Jerusalem"* The commandment is the key to this verse. The commandment means the law. When Daniel began his prayer for himself and the people of Israel he referred the commandments as the law. In Daniel 9:4 he says *"And I prayed unto the Lord my God, and made my confession, and said, O Lord, the great and dreadful God, keeping the covenant and mercy to them that love him, and to them that keep his commandments."* Also, in Exodus 20:6 it says *"And showing mercy unto thousands of them that love me, and keep my commandments."*

The first part of Daniel 9:25 was fulfilled between 458 B.C. and 25 A.D. In 458 B.C. Ezra returned to Jerusalem and there was a revival of the law[1] (*...the going forth of the commandment to restore and to build Jerusalem*). Jesus Christ was born in 5 B.C. (refer to page 5 under "Many Are Relating The Return Of Jesus Christ To The Time Of His Birth Instead Of To The Time Of His Death"). This would mean that Jesus Christ was 30 years old in 25 A.D. Jesus Christ was 30 years old when He started His earthly ministry (*... unto the Messiah the Prince*). From 458 B.C. to 25 A.D. is a total of 483 years.

The Fulfillment Of The Last Week

Jesus Christ was on the earth for 33-1/2 years. The time from the beginning of His ministry on the earth to His death was 3-1/2 years, or half of a week. This would mean that there is only a half of a week left of the seventy weeks (or 3-1/2 years) to be fulfilled.

In Daniel 9:26 it says *"And after threescore and two weeks shall Messiah be cut off, but not for himself: and the people of the prince that shall come shall destroy the city and the sanctuary; and the end thereof shall be with a flood, and unto the end of the war desolations are determined."*

During the time of his ministry Jesus Christ prophesied of the destruction of Jerusalem. In Luke 19:41-44 it says *"41 And when he was come near, he beheld the city, and wept over it, 42 Saying, If thou hadst known, even thou, at least in this thy day, the things which belong unto thy peace! but now they are hid from thine eyes. 43 For the days shall come upon thee, that thine enemies shall cast a trench about thee, and compass thee round, and keep thee in on every side, 44 And shall lay thee even with the ground, and thy children within thee; and they shall not leave in thee one stone upon another; because thou knewest not the time of thy visitation."* This prophecy was fulfilled after the death of Jesus Christ which confirms what

Daniel 9:26 said to the prophet Daniel. The destruction of the city (Jerusalem) and the sanctuary happened in 70 A.D. From 25 A.D. TO 70 A.D. is 45 years in time which is a much longer time frame to finish this prophecy of only one week or seven years left to complete.

In verse 27 Jesus Christ is the one who confirms the covenant with many. In Daniel 9:27 it says *"And he shall confirm the covenant with many for one week: and in the midst of the week he shall cause the sacrifice and the oblation to cease, and for the overspreading of abominations he shall make it desolate, even until the consummation, and that determined shall be poured upon the desolate."*

In Hebrews chapter 10 it shows that Jesus Christ through His perfect sacrifice and shed blood established the second or new covenant. In Hebrews 10:7-12 it says *"7 Then said I, Lo, I come (in the volume of the book it is written of me,) to do thy will, O God. 8 Above when he said, Sacrifice and offering and burnt offerings and offering for sin thou wouldest not, neither hadst pleasure therein; which are offered by the law; 9 Then said he, Lo, I come to do thy will, O God. He taketh away the first, that he may establish the second. 10 By the which will we are sanctified through the offering of the body of Jesus Christ once for all. 11 And every priest standeth daily ministering and offering oftentimes the same sacrifices, which can never take away sins: 12 But this man, after he had offered one sacrifice for sins for ever, sat down on the right hand of God;"*

In the second half of Daniel 9:27 there is only half of the week or 3-1/2 years still left to be fulfilled. This will be fulfilled when the Antichrist is revealed to the world (refer to page 88 "The Man Of Sin Being Revealed). The second half of Daniel 9:27 says *"and for the overspreading of abominations he shall make it desolate, even until the consummation, and that determined shall be poured upon the desolate."* Daniel 11:31 confirms that the second half of Daniel 9:27 was about the Antichrist. In Daniel 11:31 it says *"And arms shall stand on his part, and they shall pollute the sanctuary of strength, and shall take away the daily sacrifice, and they shall place the abomination that maketh desolate."* After the end of the half week or 3-1/2 years the prophecy of the seventy weeks in Daniel 9:24 will be fulfilled when the new heaven and the new earth and new Jerusalem coming down from heaven and we are ruling and reigning with Jesus Christ and God the Father for 1000 years.

CHAPTER 10

What Can A Christian Do?

For though we walk in the flesh, we do not war after the flesh: (For the weapons of our warfare are not carnal, but mighty through God to the pulling down of strong holds;) Casting down imaginations, and every high thing that exalteth itself against the knowledge of God, and bringing into captivity every thought to the obedience of Christ; II Corinthians 10:3-5

These Are The Spiritual Preparations For A Christian

You Must Be Saved

The Lord Jesus Christ spoke to Nicodemus, a religious man of his day, about being born again. Nicodemus knew about God intellectually, but he had no relationship with Him. In today's world there are many like Nicodemus who have a knowledge of God but no relationship. In John 3:1-5 it says *"1 There was a man of the Pharisees, named Nicodemus, a ruler of the Jews: 2 The same came to Jesus by night, and said unto him, Rabbi, we know that thou art a teacher come from God: for no man can do these miracles that thou doest, except God be with him. 3 Jesus answered and said unto him, Verily, verily, I say unto thee, Except a man be born again, he cannot see the kingdom of God. 4 Nicodemus saith unto him, How can a man be born when he is old? can he enter the second time into his mother's womb, and be born? 5 Jesus answered, Verily, verily, I say unto thee, Except a man be born of water and of the Spirit, he cannot enter into the kingdom of God."* In verse 4 Nicodemus was speaking of an earthly birth but in verse 3 Jesus was speaking of a heavenly birth.

The apostle Paul tells us how to be saved in Romans 10:9-10. In Romans 10:9-10 it says *"9 That if thou shalt confess with thy mouth the Lord Jesus, and shalt believe in thine heart that God hath raised him from the dead, thou shalt be saved. 10 For with the heart man believeth unto righteousness; and with the mouth confession is made unto salvation."* Paul also told us that are salvation is by grace through faith and not by our works. In Ephesians 2:8-9 it says *"8 For by grace are ye saved through faith; and that not of yourselves: it is the gift of God: 9 Not of works, lest any man should boast."*

The beginning of our relationship with Jesus Christ is when we are born again. Jesus Christ spoke to Nicodemus about this. In John 3:3 it says *"Jesus answered and said unto him, Verily, verily, I say unto thee, Except a man be born again, he cannot see the kingdom of God."*

In John 3:5 it says *"Jesus answered, Verily, verily, I say unto thee, Except a man be born of water and of the Spirit, he cannot enter into the kingdom of God."* This scripture shows an overcomer in Jesus Christ full of the word of God and being led by the Spirit of God. In Revelation chapters 2 and 3, at the end of each message to a church, Jesus spoke about the rewards that would come to those who are overcomers.

Do you know Jesus Christ as your personal saviour? If not you can repent of your sins and invite him into your heart today. To receive Jesus Christ in your heart pray this prayer out loud:

Prayer Of Salvation

Dear Lord Jesus,
I come to you as a sinner,
I know I can't make it on my own.
Forgive me for my sins,
Come into my heart,
Come into my life.
According to your Word,
In Romans 10:9-10,
You said,
That if thou shalt confess
With thy mouth the Lord Jesus,
And shalt believe in thine heart
That God hath raised Him from the dead,
Thou shalt be saved.
For with the heart,
Man believeth unto righteousness,
And with the mouth,
Confession is made unto salvation.
Thank you Lord for saving me!
I am a new creature now.
I will pray,
I will read my Bible,
I will do the things according to your Word.
In Jesus name, Amen.

You Must Receive The Baptism In The Holy Ghost

The Promise Of The Baptism In The Holy Ghost

There are many scriptures that speak about the promise of the Holy Ghost. Even John the Baptist spoke about it in Matthew 3:11. In Matthew 3:11 he said *" I indeed baptize you with water unto repentance: but he that cometh after me is mightier than I, whose shoes I am not worthy to bear: he shall baptize you with the Holy Ghost, and with fire:"* John the Baptist was saying that he baptized people in water unto repentance but Jesus Christ will baptize you with the Holy Ghost and with fire. Jesus Christ spoke many scriptures about the promise of the Holy Ghost. In John 14:16-18 Jesus said *"16 And I will pray the Father, and he shall give you another Comforter, that he may abide with you for ever; 17 Even the Spirit of truth; whom the world cannot receive, because it seeth him not, neither knoweth him: but ye know him; for he dwelleth with you, and shall be in you. 18 I will not leave you comfortless: I will come to you."* In this passage Jesus Christ spoke of giving them another Comforter. In John 14:25-26 it tells us the Comforter is the Holy Ghost. In John 14:25-26 it says *"25 These things have I spoken unto you, being yet present with you. 26 But the Comforter, which is the Holy Ghost, whom the Father will send in my name, he shall teach you all things, and bring all things to your remembrance, whatsoever I have said unto you."* Jesus told the disciples how He had to go back to the Father before the Holy Ghost could come unto them. In John 16:5-7 Jesus said *"5 But now I go my way to him that sent me; and none of you asketh me, Whither goest thou? 6 But because I have said these things unto you, sorrow hath filled your heart. 7 Nevertheless I tell you the truth; It is expedient for you that I go away: for if I go not away, the Comforter will not come unto you; but if I depart, I will send him unto you."* After Jesus rose from the dead He told them to wait for the Holy Ghost in Jerusalem. In Luke 24:49

Jesus said *"And, behold, I send the promise of my Father upon you: but tarry ye in the city of Jerusalem, until ye be endued with power from on high."* Also in Acts 1:3-5 Jesus said *"3 To whom also he shewed himself alive after his passion by many infallible proofs, being seen of them forty days, and speaking of the things pertaining to the kingdom of God: 4 And, being assembled together with them, commanded them that they should not depart from Jerusalem, but wait for the promise of the Father, which, saith he, ye have heard of me. 5 For John truly baptized with water; but ye shall be baptized with the Holy Ghost not many days hence.* And in Acts 1:8 Jesus said: *But ye shall receive power, after that the Holy Ghost is come upon you: and ye shall be witnesses unto me both in Jerusalem, and in all Judaea, and in Samaria, and unto the uttermost part of the earth."*

The Fulfillment Of The Baptism In The Holy Ghost

The promise of the Baptism in the Holy Ghost was fulfilled on the day of Pentecost. In Acts 2:1-6 it says *"1 And when the day of Pentecost was fully come, they were all with one accord in one place. 2 And suddenly there came a sound from heaven as of a rushing mighty wind, and it filled all the house where they were sitting. 3 And there appeared unto them cloven tongues like as of fire, and it sat upon each of them. 4 And they were all filled with the Holy Ghost, and began to speak with other tongues, as the Spirit gave them utterance. 5 And there were dwelling at Jerusalem Jews, devout men, out of every nation under heaven. 6 Now when this was noised abroad, the multitude came together, and were confounded, because that every man heard them speak in his own language."*

After the Holy Ghost was poured out on them the apostle Peter preached a powerful message and many were saved. In Acts 2:13-18 it says *"13 Others mocking said, These men are full of new wine. 14 But Peter, standing up with the eleven, lifted up his voice, and said unto them, Ye men of Judaea, and all ye that dwell at Jerusalem, be this known unto you, and hearken to my words: 15 For these are not drunken, as ye suppose, seeing it is but the third hour of the day. 16 But this is that which was spoken by the prophet Joel; 17 And it shall come to pass in the last days, saith God, I will pour out of my Spirit upon all flesh: and your sons and your daughters shall prophesy, and your young men shall see visions, and your old men shall dream dreams: 18 And on my servants and on my handmaidens I will pour out in those days of my Spirit; and they shall prophesy:*

After Peter had finished preaching he told the people how to be saved and filled with the Holy Ghost. In Acts 2:37-41 it says: *37 Now when they heard this, they were pricked in their heart, and said unto Peter and to the rest of the apostles, Men and brethren, what shall we do? 38 Then Peter said unto them, Repent, and be baptized every one of you in the name of Jesus Christ for the remission of sins, and ye shall receive the gift of the Holy Ghost. 39 For the promise is unto you, and to your children, and to all that are afar off, even as many as the Lord our God shall call. 40 And with many other words did he testify and exhort, saying, Save yourselves from this untoward generation. 41 Then they that gladly received his word were baptized: and the same day there were added unto them about three thousand souls."* Notice that in verses 38 and 39 that Peter said they must repent and be baptized in the name of the Lord (which is baptism in water) and *"and ye shall receive the gift of the Holy Ghost. For the promise is unto you, and to your children, and to all that are afar off, even as many as the Lord our God shall call."* This passage was not only for that day but for every Christian.

Acts 19:1-6 shows an example of people getting saved, baptized in water and receiving the Baptism in the Holy Ghost.

In Acts 19:1-6 it says *"1 And it came to pass, that, while Apollos was at Corinth, Paul having passed through the upper coasts came to Ephesus: and finding certain disciples, 2 He said unto them, Have ye received the Holy Ghost since ye believed? And they said unto him, We have not so much as heard whether there be any Holy Ghost. 3 And he said unto them, Unto what then were ye baptized? And they said, Unto John's baptism. 4 Then said Paul, John verily baptized with the baptism of repentance, saying unto the people, that they should believe on him which should come after him, that is, on Christ Jesus. 5 When they heard this, they were baptized in the name of the Lord Jesus. 6 And when Paul had laid his hands upon them, the Holy Ghost came on them; and they spake with tongues, and prophesied."*

In Acts 8:14-17 it says *"14 Now when the apostles which were at Jerusalem heard that Samaria had received the word of God, they sent unto them Peter and John: 15 Who, when they were come down, prayed for them, that they might receive the Holy Ghost: 16 (For as yet he was fallen upon none of them: only they were baptized in the name of the Lord Jesus.) 17 Then laid they their hands on them, and they received the Holy Ghost."*

If you have not received the baptism in the Holy Ghost, pray that Jesus Christ would baptize you now in the Holy Ghost. In Luke 11:13 Jesus says *"If ye then, being evil, know how to give good gifts unto your children: how much more shall your heavenly Father give the Holy Spirit to them that ask him?"* Also in Acts 5:32 the Holy Ghost is given to them that obey him. Acts 5:32 says *"And we are his witnesses of these things; and so is also the Holy Ghost, whom God hath given to them that obey him."*

You Must Put The Word Of God In Your Heart

So many Christians in America do not have the word of God in their hearts. We need to compare ourselves with the persecuted church around the world. The word of God is very precious to Christians in countries where they are persecuted. The Bible is so precious to them that when they have any portion of the Holy Bible they memorize it, study it and put the word of God in their hearts , so even if their Bible is taken from them the Word of God can not be taken out of their hearts. How important it is that we treat the Word of God with the same respect. David said in Psalm 119:11 it says *"Thy word have I hid in mine heart, that I might not sin against thee."*

Many Christians receive the Baptism in the Holy Ghost, but there is no power in their lives. Unlike the disciples, most Christians who are filled with the Holy Ghost cannot cast out devils, pray for the sick to be healed, or pray for the dead to be raised. The Lord Jesus told me why the disciples, after they were filled with the Holy Ghost, walked in power, and today's Christian don't. He said it is because for 3-1/2 years the disciples heard the word of God from Jesus.   After they received the Holy Ghost the power of God was manifested through them. Jesus spoke about having the Word of God in your heart. In John 15:1-7 He said *"1 I am the true vine, and my Father is the husbandman. 2 Every branch in me that beareth not fruit he taketh away: and every branch that beareth fruit, he purgeth it, that it may bring forth more fruit. 3 Now ye are clean through the word which I have spoken unto you. 4 Abide in me, and I in you. As the branch cannot bear fruit of itself, except it abide in the vine; no more can ye, except ye abide in me. 5 I am the vine, ye are the branches: He that abideth in me, and I in him, the same bringeth forth much fruit: for without me ye can do nothing. 6 If a man abide not in me, he is cast forth as a branch, and is withered; and men gather them, and cast them into the fire, and they are burned. 7 If ye abide in me, and my words abide in you, ye shall ask what ye will, and it shall be done unto you.* "Also in John 8:31 Jesus said *"Then said Jesus to those Jews which believed on him, If ye continue in my word, then are ye my disciples indeed."*

Jesus Christ provided us with an example of how to have victory over the devil using the Word of God in our hearts. In Matthew 4:1-11 it says *"1 Then was Jesus led up of the Spirit into the wilderness to be tempted of the devil. 2 And when he had fasted forty days and forty nights, he was afterward an hungred. 3 And when the tempter came to him, he said, If thou be the Son of God, command that these stones be made bread. 4 But he answered and said, It is written, Man shall not live by bread alone, but by every word that proceedeth out of the mouth of God. 5 Then the devil taketh him up into the holy city, and setteth him on a pinnacle of the temple, 6 And saith unto him, If thou be the Son of God, cast thyself down: for it is written, He shall give his angels charge concerning thee: and in their hands they shall bear thee up, lest at any time thou dash thy foot against a stone. 7 Jesus said unto him, It is written again, Thou shalt not tempt the Lord thy God. 8 Again, the devil taketh him up into an exceeding high mountain, and sheweth him all the kingdoms of the world, and the glory of them; 9 And saith unto him, All these things will I give thee, if thou wilt fall down and worship me. 10 Then saith Jesus unto him, Get thee hence, Satan: for it is written, Thou shalt worship the Lord thy God, and him only shalt thou serve. 11 Then the devil leaveth him, and, behold, angels came and ministered unto him."* Jesus Christ, the Son of God, had the Word of God in His heart and was victorious over the devil.

Do you have the Word of God in your heart? If your Bible was taken today could you live a life of victory with the scriptures that are in your heart? If your answer is no, then here are some scriptures to help you start memorizing the Holy Bible. I encourage you to put the following scriptures in your heart: John 3:16, Romans 10:9-10, Psalm 119:11, James 4:17, I John 1:9, Ephesians 2:8-9, John 10:29, I Corinthians 10:13, I Peter 2:2, II Corinthians 5:17, Hebrews 11:1, Hosea 4:6, Romans 10:17, James 1:14, II Timothy 2:15, Isaiah 26:3, Hebrews 11:6, Psalm 34:1, James 1:5 and Isaiah 53:5.

You Must Pray In The Gift Of Tongues And In English Daily

Praying In The Gift Of Tongues

Many Christians receive the Baptism in the Holy Ghost and begin to pray in tongues but after that initial experience they stop praying in tongues. We must pray in tongues daily. In I Corinthians 14:18 Paul said *" I thank my God, I speak with tongues more than ye all:"* We also know that praying in tongues builds us up spiritually. In Jude 20 it says *"But ye, beloved, building up yourselves on your most holy faith, praying in the Holy Ghost,"* Also, in I Corinthians 14:4 it says *"He that speaketh in an unknown tongue edifieth himself; but he that prophesieth edifieth the church."*

When we pray in tongues we are speaking to God. In I Corinthians 14:2 it says *"For he that speaketh in an unknown tongue speaketh not unto men, but unto God: for no man understandeth him; howbeit in the spirit he speaketh mysteries."* Also in Romans 8:26-27 it says *"26 Likewise the Spirit also helpeth our infirmities: for we know not what we should pray for as we ought: but the Spirit itself maketh intercession for us with groanings which cannot be uttered. 27 And he that searcheth the hearts knoweth what is the mind of the Spirit, because he maketh intercession for the saints according to the will of God."* When you are praying in tongues you can only pray the will of God. If we pray the will of God we know that are prayers will be answered. In I John 5:14-15 it says *"14 And this is the confidence that we have in him, that, if we ask any thing according to his will, he heareth us: 15 And if we know that he hear us, whatsoever we ask, we know that we have the petitions that we desired of him."*

Praying In English

Many Christians know how to pray but just don't take the time to do it. Prayer is one of the most important parts of your relationship with Jesus Christ. How can you have a true relationship with Jesus Christ if you never spend time with the Lord? Many are so busy for Jesus that they have missed the most important part of their relationship with Him and that is getting to know the Saviour. Jesus Christ and the apostles spoke many times about prayer. In Luke 18:1 it says *"And he spake a parable unto them to this end, that men ought always to pray, and not to faint;"* The apostle Paul spoke in Philippians 4:6 about prayer. In Philippians 4:6 *"Be careful for nothing; but in every thing by prayer and supplication with thanksgiving let your requests be made known unto God."* Also the apostles give us many examples of prayer in the first church. In Acts 6:1-4 it says *"1 And in those days, when the number of the disciples was multiplied, there arose a murmuring of the Grecians against the Hebrews, because their widows were neglected in the daily ministration. 2 Then the twelve called the multitude of the disciples unto them, and said, It is not reason that we should leave the word of God, and serve tables. 3 Wherefore, brethren, look ye out among you seven men of honest report, full of the Holy Ghost and wisdom, whom we may appoint over this business. 4 But we will give ourselves continually to prayer, and to the ministry of the word."*

You Must Know The Voice Of Jesus Christ

When you pray for God's leading, you must wait for the answer from Jesus Christ. The only way to know if we have received the answer is to know God's voice. In the gospel of John, Jesus speaks of Christians as sheep. He tells us that "My sheep hear My voice and I know them and they follow me." In John 10:1-14 Jesus says *"1 Verily, verily, I say unto you, He that entereth not by the door into the sheepfold, but climbeth up some other way, the same is a thief and a robber. 2 But he that entereth in by the door is the shepherd of the sheep. 3 To him the porter openeth; and the sheep hear his voice: and he calleth his own sheep by name, and leadeth them out. 4 And when he putteth forth his own sheep, he goeth before them, and the sheep follow him: for they know his voice. 5 And a stranger will they not follow, but will flee from him: for they know not the voice of strangers. 6 This parable spake Jesus unto them: but they understood not what things they were which he spake unto them. 7 Then said Jesus unto them again, Verily, verily, I say unto you, I am the door of the sheep. 8 All that ever came before me are thieves and robbers: but the sheep did not hear them. 9 I am the door: by me if any man enter in, he shall be saved, and shall go in and out, and find pasture. 10 The thief cometh not, but for to steal, and to kill, and to destroy: I am come that they might have life, and that they might have it more abundantly. 11 I am the good shepherd: the good shepherd giveth his life for the sheep. 12 But he that is an hireling, and not the shepherd, whose own the sheep are not, seeth the wolf coming, and leaveth the sheep, and fleeth: and the wolf catcheth them, and scattereth the sheep. 13 The hireling fleeth, because he is an hireling, and careth not for the sheep. 14 I am the good shepherd, and know my sheep, and am known of mine.* Notice in verse 5 that the sheep (which is symbolic of a Christian) will not follow the voice of strangers. In John 10:5 it says *"And a stranger will they not follow, but will flee from him: for they know not the voice of strangers."*

John 10:27-28 says *27 My sheep hear my voice, and I know them, and they follow me: 28 And I give unto them eternal life; and they shall never perish, neither shall any man pluck them out of my hand."* We are entering into the most demonic times the world has ever seen. Do you know the voice of Jesus Christ? Your spiritual life will depend on it.

Three Example Of Hearing God's Voice

Jesus Christ - The Perfect Example

The Lord Jesus Christ shows us the perfect example one who hears God's voice. He always did exactly what was asked of Him by the Father. We see this example in John 8:26-29. In John 8:26-29 it says *"26 I have many things to say and to judge of you: but he that sent me is true; and I speak to the world those things which I have heard of him. 27 They understood not that he spake to them of the Father. 28 Then said Jesus unto them, When ye have lifted up the Son of man, then shall ye know that I am he, and that I do nothing of myself; but as my Father hath taught me, I speak these things. 29 And he that sent me is with me: the Father hath not left me alone; for I do always those things that please him."*

Jonah - One Who Disobeyed And Later Repented

In the book of Jonah we see how after God spoke Jonah to go to Nineveh and cry against it. Jonah disobeyed and ran from the Lord. In Jonah 1:1-17 it says *"1 Now the word of the LORD came unto Jonah the son of Amittai, saying, 2 Arise, go to Nineveh, that great city, and cry against it; for their wickedness is come up before me. 3 But Jonah rose up to flee unto Tarshish* from the presence of the LORD, and went down to Joppa; and he found a ship going to Tarshish: so he paid the fare thereof, and went down into it, to go with them unto Tarshish from the presence of the LORD. 4 But the LORD sent out a great wind into the sea, and there was a mighty tempest in the sea, so that the ship was like to be broken. 5 Then the mariners were afraid, and cried every man unto his god, and cast forth the wares that were in the ship into the sea, to lighten it of them. But Jonah was gone down into the sides of the ship; and he lay, and was fast asleep. 6 So the shipmaster came to him, and said unto him, What meanest thou, O sleeper? arise, call upon thy God, if so be that God will think upon us, that we perish not. 7 And they said every one to his fellow, Come, and let us cast lots, that we may know for whose cause this evil is upon us. So they cast lots, and the lot fell upon Jonah. 8 Then said they unto him, Tell us, we pray thee, for whose cause this evil is upon us; What is thine occupation? and whence comest thou? what is thy country? and of what people art thou? 9 And he said unto them, I am an Hebrew; and I fear the LORD, the God of heaven, which hath made the sea and the dry land. 10 Then were the men exceedingly afraid, and said unto him, Why hast thou done this? For the men knew that he fled from the presence of the LORD, because he had told them. 11 Then said they unto him, What shall we do unto thee, that the sea may be calm unto us? for the sea wrought, and was tempestuous. 12 And he said unto them, Take me up, and cast me forth into the sea; so shall the sea be calm unto you: for I know that for my sake this great tempest is upon you. 13 Nevertheless the men rowed hard to bring it to the land; but they could not: for the sea wrought, and was tempestuous against them. 14 Wherefore they cried unto the LORD, and said, We beseech thee, O LORD, we beseech thee, let us not perish for this man's life, and lay not upon us innocent blood: for thou, O LORD, hast done as it pleased thee. 15 So they took up Jonah, and cast him forth into the sea: and the sea ceased from her raging. 16 Then the men feared the

LORD exceedingly, and offered a sacrifice unto the LORD, and made vows. 17 Now the LORD had prepared a great fish to swallow up Jonah. And Jonah was in the belly of the fish three days and three nights."

After the prophet Jonah disobeyed God the Lord prepared a place for Jonah to repent. This place was in the belly of the great fish that swallowed him. In Jonah 2:1-10 it says *"1 Then Jonah prayed unto the LORD his God out of the fish's belly, 2 And said, I cried by reason of mine affliction unto the LORD, and he heard me; out of the belly of hell cried I, and thou heardest my voice. 3 For thou hadst cast me into the deep, in the midst of the seas; and the floods compassed me about: all thy billows and thy waves passed over me. 4 Then I said, I am cast out of thy sight; yet I will look again toward thy holy temple. 5 The waters compassed me about, even to the soul: the depth closed me round about, the weeds were wrapped about my head. 6 I went down to the bottoms of the mountains; the earth with her bars was about me for ever: yet hast thou brought up my life from corruption, O LORD my God. 7 When my soul fainted within me I remembered the LORD: and my prayer came in unto thee, into thine holy temple. 8 They that observe lying vanities forsake their own mercy. 9 But I will sacrifice unto thee with the voice of thanksgiving; I will pay that that I have vowed. Salvation is of the LORD. 10 And the LORD spake unto the fish, and it vomited out Jonah upon the dry land."*

After Jonah repented God spoke to him again to preach to Nineveh. This time Jonah obeyed and did what the Lord told him to do. We see this in Jonah 3:1-10 which says *"1 And the word of the LORD came unto Jonah the second time, saying, 2 Arise, go unto Nineveh, that great city, and preach unto it the preaching that I bid thee. 3 So Jonah arose, and went unto Nineveh, according to the word of the LORD. Now Nineveh was* an exceeding great city of three days' journey. *4 And Jonah began to enter into the city a day's journey, and he cried, and said, Yet forty days, and Nineveh shall be overthrown. 5 So the people of Nineveh believed God, and proclaimed a fast, and put on sackcloth, from the greatest of them even to the least of them. 6 For word came unto the king of Nineveh, and he arose from his throne, and he laid his robe from him, and covered him with sackcloth, and sat in ashes. 7 And he caused it to be proclaimed and published through Nineveh by the decree of the king and his nobles, saying, Let neither man nor beast, herd nor flock, taste any thing: let them not feed, nor drink water: 8 But let man and beast be covered with sackcloth, and cry mightily unto God: yea, let them turn every one from his evil way, and from the violence that is in their hands. 9 Who can tell if God will turn and repent, and turn away from his fierce anger, that we perish not? 10 And God saw their works, that they turned from their evil way; and God repented of the evil, that he had said that he would do unto them; and he did it not."* Through the obedience of the prophet Jonah, Nineveh repented and God did not destroy it.

Saul - One Who Disobeyed And Lost His Soul

This is an example of what no one wants to be. King Saul heard the instructions from the Lord, but he chose to disobey the Lord, and it cost him his soul. In I Samuel 15:1-24 it says *"1 Samuel also said unto Saul, The LORD sent me to anoint thee to be king over his people, over Israel: now therefore hearken thou unto the voice of the words of the LORD. 2 Thus saith the LORD of hosts, I remember that which Amalek did to Israel, how he laid wait for him in the way, when he came up from Egypt. 3 Now go and smite Amalek, and utterly destroy all that they have, and spare them not; but slay both man and woman, infant and suckling, ox and sheep, camel and ass. 4 And Saul gathered the people together, and numbered them in Telaim, two hundred thousand footmen, and ten thousand men of Judah. 5 And Saul came to a city of Amalek, and laid wait in the valley. 6 And Saul said unto the Kenites, Go, depart, get you down from among the Amalekites, lest I destroy you with them: for ye shewed kindness to all the children of Israel, when they came up out of Egypt. So the Kenites departed from among the Amalekites. 7 And Saul smote the Amalekites from Havilah until thou comest to Shur, that is over against Egypt. 8 And he took Agag the king of the Amalekites alive, and utterly destroyed all the people with the edge of the sword. 9 But Saul and the people spared Agag, and the best of the sheep, and of the oxen, and of the fatlings, and the lambs, and all that was good, and would not utterly destroy them: but every thing that was vile and refuse, that they destroyed utterly. 10 Then came the word of the LORD unto Samuel, saying, 11 It repenteth me that I have set up Saul to be king: for he is turned back from following me, and hath not performed my commandments. And it grieved Samuel; and he cried unto the LORD all night. 12 And when Samuel rose early to meet Saul in the morning, it was told Samuel, saying, Saul came to Carmel, and, behold, he set him up a place, and is gone about, and passed on, and gone down to Gilgal. 13 And Samuel came to Saul: and Saul said unto him, Blessed be thou of the LORD: I have performed the commandment of the LORD. 14 And Samuel said, What meaneth then this bleating of the sheep in mine ears, and the lowing of the oxen which I hear? 15 And Saul said, They have brought them from the Amalekites: for the people spared the best of the sheep and of the oxen, to sacrifice unto the LORD thy God; and the rest we have utterly destroyed. 16 Then Samuel said unto Saul, Stay, and I will tell thee what the LORD hath said to me this night. And he said unto him, Say on. 17 And Samuel said, When thou wast little in thine own sight, wast thou not made the head of the tribes of Israel, and the LORD anointed thee king over Israel? 18 And the LORD sent thee on a journey, and said, Go and utterly destroy the sinners the*

Amalekites, and fight against them until they be consumed. 19 Wherefore then didst thou not obey the voice of the LORD, but didst fly upon the spoil, and didst evil in the sight of the LORD? 20 And Saul said unto Samuel, Yea, I have obeyed the voice of the LORD, and have gone the way which the LORD sent me, and have brought Agag the king of Amalek, and have utterly destroyed the Amalekites. 21 But the people took of the spoil, sheep and oxen, the chief of the things which should have been utterly destroyed, to sacrifice unto the LORD thy God in Gilgal. 22 And Samuel said, Hath the LORD as great delight in burnt offerings and sacrifices, as in obeying the voice of the LORD? Behold, to obey is better than sacrifice, and to hearken than the fat of rams. 23 For rebellion is as the sin of witchcraft, and stubbornness is as iniquity and idolatry. Because thou hast rejected the word of the LORD, he hath also rejected thee from being king. 24 And Saul said unto Samuel, I have sinned: for I have transgressed the commandment of the LORD, and thy words: because I feared the people, and obeyed their voice." King Saul feared the people more than he did the Lord and lost his soul. In I Chronicles 10:13-14 it says *"13 So Saul died for his transgression which he committed against the LORD, even against the word of the LORD, which he kept not, and also for asking counsel of one that had a familiar spirit, to enquire of it; 14 And enquired not of the LORD: therefore he slew him, and turned the kingdom unto David the son of Jesse."*

You Must Study The Word Of God

We must not only put the word of God in our hearts, but we must also know how to find the scriptures in the Holy Bible. The apostle Paul shows us this in II Timothy 2:15. This verse says *"15 Study to shew thyself approved unto God, a workman that needeth not to be ashamed, rightly dividing the word of truth."* Jesus Christ told those who believed on him to continue in His word. In John 8:31-32 it says *"31 Then said Jesus to those Jews which believed on him, If ye continue in my word, then are ye my disciples indeed; 32 And ye shall know the truth, and the truth shall make you free."* Also in I Peter 2:2 it says *"2 As newborn babes, desire the sincere milk of the word, that ye may grow thereby:"* The apostle Peter shows us an example of what Paul told us in II Timothy 2:15. In I Peter 3:15 it says *"But sanctify the Lord God in your hearts: and be ready always to give an answer to every man that asketh you a reason of the hope that is in you with meekness and fear:"* We as Christians must be able to share our faith in Jesus Christ and we must also be able show the lost sinner what we are saying is in God's Holy Bible.

You Must Let The Holy Ghost Lead You

Many Christians who have received the Baptism in the Holy Ghost are not led by the Spirit of God. Notice what Jesus says in John 14:26 and in John 16:13-15. In John 14:26 Jesus says *"26 But the Comforter, which is the Holy Ghost, whom the Father will send in my name, he shall teach you all things, and bring all things to your remembrance, whatsoever I have said unto you."* And in John 16:13-15 it says *"13 Howbeit when he, the Spirit of truth, is come, he will guide you into all truth: for he shall not speak of himself; but whatsoever he shall hear, that shall he speak: and he will shew you things to come. 14 He shall glorify me: for he shall receive of mine, and shall shew it unto you. 15 All things that the Father hath are mine: therefore said I, that he shall take of mine, and shall shew it unto you."* The Holy Ghost wants to lead us but we have to let him.

Three Examples Of Being Led By The Holy Ghost

Jesus Christ

After Jesus was baptized in water by John the Baptist in the river Jordan. Then the Spirit of God descended on him like a dove and God spoke from Heaven. The Bible says that after this Jesus Christ was led of the Spirit into the wilderness to be tempted of the devil. In Matthew 4:1 it says *" Then was Jesus led up of the Spirit into the wilderness to be tempted of the devil. "*

The capital letter S used in the word "Spirit" in Matthew 4:1 is speaking of the Holy Ghost. We can confirm this with other scriptures in the Bible. In John 14:16-17 it says *"16 And I will pray the Father, and he shall give you another Comforter, that he may abide with you for ever; 17 Even the Spirit of truth; whom the world cannot receive, because it seeth him not, neither knoweth him: but ye know him; for he dwelleth with you, and shall be in you."* In John 14:26 it says *" But the Comforter, which is the Holy Ghost, whom the Father will send in my name, he shall teach you all things, and bring all things to your remembrance, whatsoever I have said unto you."* In John 15:26 it says *"26 But when the Comforter is come, whom I will send unto you from the Father, even the Spirit of truth, which proceedeth from the Father, he shall testify of me:"* From these verses we see that the Comforter which is the Holy Ghost is also the Spirit of truth which confirms that when the Bible speaks of the Spirit (with a capital S) it is speaking of the Holy Ghost.

Peter

In the book of Acts chapter 10, the Bible tells us how Jesus Christ had to prepare the apostle Peter to preach to the Gentile people. In Acts 10:9-16 It says *"9 On the morrow, as they went on their journey, and drew nigh unto the city, Peter went up upon the housetop to pray about the sixth hour: 10 And he became very hungry, and would have eaten: but while they made ready, he fell into a trance, 11 And saw heaven opened, and a certain vessel descending unto him, as it had been a great sheet knit at the four corners, and let down to the earth: 12 Wherein were all manner of fourfooted beasts of the earth, and wild beasts, and creeping things, and fowls of the air. 13 And there came a voice to him, Rise, Peter; kill, and eat. 14 But Peter said, Not so, Lord; for I have never eaten any thing that is common or unclean. 15 And the voice spake unto him again the second time, What God hath cleansed, that call not thou common. 16 This was done thrice: and the vessel was received up again into heaven."* Through this trance Peter had, God was preparing him to meet three Gentiles.

In Acts 10:17-22 it says *" 17 Now while Peter doubted in himself what this vision which he had seen should mean, behold, the men which were sent from Cornelius had made enquiry for Simon's house, and stood before the gate, 18 And called, and asked whether Simon, which was surnamed Peter, were lodged there. 19 While Peter thought on the vision, the Spirit said unto him, Behold, three men seek thee. 20 Arise therefore, and get thee down, and go with them, doubting nothing: for I have sent them. 21 Then Peter went down to the men which were sent unto him from Cornelius; and said, Behold, I am he whom ye seek: what is the cause wherefore ye are come? 22 And they said, Cornelius the centurion, a just man, and one that feareth God, and of good report among all the nation of the Jews, was warned from God by an holy angel to send for thee into his house, and to hear words of thee."* While Peter thought on the vision, the Spirit, or the Holy Ghost spoke to him and told him "three men seek thee." The Holy Spirit told Peter to go with these men. Peter obeyed the Lord and went to Cornelius to preach Jesus to him and his household. In Acts 10:34-45 it says *"34 Then Peter opened his mouth, and said, Of a truth I perceive that God is no respecter of persons: 35 But in every nation he that feareth him, and worketh righteousness, is accepted with him. 36 The word which God sent unto the children of Israel, preaching peace by Jesus Christ: (he is Lord of all:) 37 That word, I say, ye know, which was published throughout all Judaea, and began from Galilee, after the baptism which John preached; 38 How God anointed Jesus of Nazareth with the Holy Ghost and with power: who went about doing good, and healing all that were oppressed of the devil; for God was with him. 39 And we are witnesses of all things which he did both in the land of the Jews, and in Jerusalem; whom they slew and hanged on a tree: 40 Him God raised up the third day, and shewed him openly; 41 Not to all the people, but unto witnesses chosen before of God, even to us, who did eat and drink with him after he rose from the dead. 42 And he commanded us to preach unto the people, and to testify that it is he which was ordained of God to be the Judge of quick and dead. 43 To him give all the prophets witness, that through his name whosoever believeth in him shall receive remission of sins. 44 While Peter yet spake these words, the Holy Ghost fell on all them which heard the word. 45 And they of the circumcision which believed were astonished, as many as came with Peter, because that on the Gentiles also was poured out the gift of the Holy Ghost."* By the apostle Peter letting the Holy Ghost lead him the Holy Ghost was poured on the Gentiles for the first time.

Paul

The apostle Paul was one of the greatest apostles to ever live on the earth and Paul wrote many books in the new testament. Paul also wrote about being led by the Spirit of God. Acts 16:6-10 shows how the Holy Ghost led him to Macedonia. In Acts

16:6-10 it says *"6 Now when they had gone throughout Phrygia and the region of Galatia, and were forbidden of the Holy Ghost to preach the word in Asia, 7 After they were come to Mysia, they assayed to go into Bithynia: but the Spirit suffered them not. 8 And they passing by Mysia came down to Troas. 9 And a vision appeared to Paul in the night; There stood a man of Macedonia, and prayed him, saying, Come over into Macedonia, and help us. 10 And after he had seen the vision, immediately we endeavoured to go into Macedonia, assuredly gathering that the Lord had called us for to preach the gospel unto them."*

We see from these three examples of being led by the Spirit of God that we must be mature in the word of God and very sensitive to the leading of the Holy Ghost.

These Are The Physical Preparations for a Christian

Without the spiritual preparations you will not be prepared even with lots of food. We must first get our spiritual house in order before the physical preparations will be of any help.

1. Food Storage and Water Preparations

Here are some scriptures that show God's people making physical preparations. In Luke 17:26-27 Jesus says *"26 And as it was in the days of Noe, so shall it be also in the days of the Son of man. 27 They did eat, they drank, they married wives, they were given in marriage, until the day that Noe entered into the ark, and the flood came, and destroyed them all."* We know in the days of Noah, Noah prepared food in the ark. In Genesis 6:21-22 it says *"21 And take thou unto thee of all food that is eaten, and thou shalt gather it to thee; and it shall be for food for thee, and for them. 22 Thus did Noah; according to all that God commanded him, so did he."*

God used Joseph in Egypt to interpret Pharaoh's dream and to store food in the seven years of plenty before the seven years of famine. Genesis 41:28-31 says *"28 This is the thing which I have spoken unto Pharaoh: What God is about to do he sheweth unto Pharaoh. 29 Behold, there come seven years of great plenty throughout all the land of Egypt: 30 And there shall arise after them seven years of famine; and all the plenty shall be forgotten in the land of Egypt; and the famine shall consume the land; 31 And the plenty shall not be known in the land by reason of that famine following; for it shall be very grievous.*

Genesis 41:46-49 says *"46 And Joseph was thirty years old when he stood before Pharaoh king of Egypt. And Joseph went out from the presence of Pharaoh, and went throughout all the land of Egypt. 47 And in the seven plenteous years the earth brought forth by handfuls. 48 And he gathered up all the food of the seven years, which were in the land of Egypt, and laid up the food in the cities: the food of the field, which was round about every city, laid he up in the same. 49 And Joseph gathered corn as the sand of the sea, very much, until he left numbering; for it was without number."*

In Acts 11:28-29 the prophet Agabus prophesied great dearth (which means scarcity) throughout the world and they sent relief to the brethren in Judaea. In Acts 11:28-29 it says *"28 And there stood up one of them named Agabus, and signified by the Spirit that there should be great dearth throughout all the world: which came to pass in the days of Claudius Caesar. 29 Then the disciples, every man according to his ability, determined to send relief unto the brethren which dwelt in Judaea: 30 Which also they did, and sent it to the elders by the hands of Barnabas and Saul."* From these passages of scriptures we see God did tell His people to prepare for difficult times on the earth.

Here is a list which contains suggestions for food and water items which you can store. These items and quantities are just suggestions. For your individual situation you must pray and seek the Lord Jesus Christ on what you need to do.

FOODS (Type of foods, mostly dried, some canned)

Type	Item	Lbs
Beans	Lentil	75
	Pinto	50
Beverages	Herb tea	5
	Peppermint tea	1
Cereal	Cream of wheat	5
	Oatmeal	100
Flour	Corn meal	125
	White flour	250
Fruit	Prunes	25
	Raisins	25
Infant foods	Children's dried fruits	7
	Infant milk powder	25
Leavening	Baking powder	30
	Yeast	10
Meat/Fish	Canned corned beef	25
	Canned pink salmon	25

| Milk | Milk powder | 75 |
| | Powdered buttermilk | 50 |

| Misc. | Apple cider vinegar | 8 |
| | Powdered butter | 3 |

Type	**Item**	**Lbs**
Oil	Mazola corn oil	25
	Olive oil	25
Salt	Iodized salt	100
Seasoning	Garlic powder	7
	Chili powder	1
Small Meals	Canned Soup	50
	Cup of Noodle	5
Starch	Potato Flakes	25
	Rice (Brown/White)	100
Sugar	Brown Sugar	100
	White Sugar	100
Vegetable	Vegetable Seeds (sprouts)	4
Herbs	Kelp Granules (a natural source of iodine)	20

Food Storage

To store your food items:

1) remove food items from boxes and store in plastic bags with a plastic zipper type closure.

2)Store these bags in doubled plastic garbage bags (ex. 45 gallon size).
3)Store the garbage bags in use galvanized steel garbage cans (32 gallon).
4)Seal plastic bags and put garbage can lid on top.

Drinking Water
Store water in clean plastic water containers (5 gallon and 1 gallon sizes - the type that you buy distilled water in at the grocery store).   Do not use plastic containers that have previously contained something else. (Replace your water every 6 months).

Also, set up a water purification system (ex. boiling, filtered systems).

Water For Other Uses
Store in 32 gallon plastic garbage cans with lids.

2. Becoming Self-Sufficient

In the book of Acts we see the church responding to all the needs of the body of Christ. In Acts 2:42-47 it says *"42 And they continued stedfastly in the apostles' doctrine and fellowship, and in breaking of bread, and in prayers. 43 And fear came upon every soul: and many wonders and signs were done by the apostles. 44 And all that believed were together, and had all things common; 45 And sold their possessions and goods, and parted them to all men, as every man had need. 46 And they, continuing daily with one accord in the temple, and breaking bread from house to house, did eat their meat with gladness and singleness of heart, 47 Praising God, and having favour with all the people. And the Lord added to the church daily such as should be saved."*

Also, in Acts 4:32-37 it says *"32 And the multitude of them that believed were of one heart and of one soul: neither said any of them that ought of the things which he possessed was his own; but they had all things common 33 And with great power gave the apostles witness of the resurrection of the Lord Jesus: and great grace was upon them all. 34 Neither was there any among them that lacked: for as many as were possessors of lands or houses sold them, and brought the prices of the things that were sold, 35 And laid them down at the apostles' feet: and distribution was made unto every man according as he had need. 36 And Joses, who by the apostles was surnamed Barnabas, (which is, being interpreted, The son of consolation,) a Levite, and of the country of Cyprus, 37 Having land, sold it, and brought the money, and laid it at the apostles' feet."*

Learn to become more self-sufficient. Learn how to make your own soap, shampoos and other skin care products. Send a self-addressed stamped envelope to:

The Franklin and Franklin Company
P.O. Box 6271
Vancouver, WA 98668

Request information about Making Good Scents(TM).

Or visit the website at: makinggoodscents.com

References

CHAPTER 1
1. Riplinger, G.A., New Age Bible Versions, (Ararat, Virginia: A.V. Publications Corp., 1993), p.28.

2. Unger, Merrill F., Unger's Bible Dictionary, (Chicago, Illinois: Moody Bible Press,
1985), p. 485.

CHAPTER 2
1. Southwest Radio Church, February 1998, L-834 (P.O. Box 1144, Oklahoma City, Oklahoma 73101), p.3.

CHAPTER 4
1. All definitions taken from Webster's New World Dictionary and Unger's Bible Dictionary.

CHAPTER 9
1. Unger, Merrill F., Unger's Bible Dictionary, (Chicago, Illinois: Moody Bible Press,
1985), p. 491.

NOTES

NOTES